YO-BUP-159

920.073
B96t
1970

73 -63

Busch, Niven, 1903–
   Twenty-one Americans; being profiles of some people famous in our time, together with silly pictures of them drawn by De Miskey. Freeport, N. Y., Books for Libraries Press ₁1970, °1930₁

   vi, 332 p. illus. 23 cm. (Essay index reprint series)

1. U. S.—Biography.   ɪ. Title.

E747.B97   1970   917.3′03′910922
SBN 8369–1552–6

1275
72–99686
MARC

Library of Con

TWENTY-ONE AMERICANS

TWENTY-ONE AMERICANS

Being Profiles of Some People Famous in
Our Time, Together With Silly Pictures
of Them Drawn by De Miskey

BY
NIVEN BUSCH, Jr.

Essay Index Reprint Series

 BOOKS FOR LIBRARIES PRESS
FREEPORT, NEW YORK

Copyright © 1927, 1928, 1929, 1930 by Niven Busch, Jr.

Reprinted 1970 by arrangement
with Doubleday & Company, Inc.

920.073
B96t
1970
73-63

San Francisco Public Library

STANDARD BOOK NUMBER:
8369-1552-6

LIBRARY OF CONGRESS CATALOG CARD NUMBER:
72-99686

PRINTED IN THE UNITED STATES OF AMERICA

CONTENTS

v

CONTENTS

TURKEY IN THE STRAW

TURKEY IN THE STRAW

HENRY FORD'S face looks different from every angle. Seeing him full-face you would not suspect the sharpness and delicacy of his profile, the long nose and hard chin, and if you had seen him only in profile you might not recognize, if he were sitting straight across from you, the small head, the wide, strong, thin, uneven mouth, the lank, thoughtful line of the cheeks. His face is divided between the eyebrows by a small seam which might be also the dividing line of his character, for the right side of the face is not a duplicate of the left. There are more lines in the left side; it seems kindlier, shrewder, and less firm than the right side, as if through the gray eyes two separate men looked out. Only one quality belongs to the face as a whole, a waiting quality, something birdlike and attentive, as if the consciousness that perches, light as a bird, behind the aging face, were always trying to hear something, to guess something.

It is as hard to estimate Henry Ford from the things he has done as it is to guess his nature from his face. First of all he is a mechanic, but he is also a lot more. Out of the part of his mind that with increasing leisure has turned from concrete things to abstractions have come many projects and ambitions—the Peace Ship, the attack on the Jews, a hospital, an airport, the *Dearborn Independent,* the Ford-for-President clubs. Out of the part that is formidable and characteristic has come a new automobile.

Literally, of course, a man's mind cannot be divided into separate parts any more than his face can. In Henry Ford the mechanic is the unit that knits up his multiple personalities. Giving away one of his violent pamphlets against the Jews he once said proudly: "This came out of our factory."

In this satisfaction at being a workman he always remembers that until he was nearly forty he depended on his own tools for a living. Loyal to his past, he makes brothers of all mechanics and gives them liberties he would refuse anyone else. In 1923 he was outlining his political ideas to some reporters when the door of his office opened and a man in oil-stained overalls looked in.

"What is it?" Ford called. The mechanic said: "That engine's going, Mr. Ford." Ford got up. "Gentlemen, you will have to excuse me."

When he has his hair cut he likes to delay in the chair, talking to the Dearborn barber. Cards are sometimes set in the barber's window announcing

an auction at some farm near Dearborn. Ford has
been known to take an afternoon off and go to one
of these auctions, where he strolls around, chatting
with the farmers. He talks the way they do, with
the same gift for spitting silences and thoughts re-
duced to apothegm.

"I believe in religion but I don't work at it much."

"A man who offers charity offers insult."

"It is my ambition to abolish poverty."

"Literature is all right, but it doesn't mean much."

He swears moderately in ordinary conversation
and vehemently when excited. Except for pamphlets
on engineering, he reads very little; he has forgotten
most of the things he learned in the Scotch settlement
school near his father's farm, and this scorn for
conventional education is often cited as one more
proof of the originality of his mind. It has not always been an advantage to him. When he was suing
the Chicago *Tribune* for libel, his lawyers heard that
the opposing counsel were going to examine him on
history. For three days in a room in the Blackstone
Hotel they crammed him with facts about the life
of Washington, the annexation of Florida, the battle
of Bull Run, and the Dingley tariff. That he failed
on the stand was not due to lack of coaching but to
the fact that his tutors had overlooked certain
simpler questions.

"Who was Benedict Arnold?" asked the lawyer for the *Tribune,* bowing blandly toward the manufacturer, who sat in an awkward position in the witness chair with his long legs crossed and his hands clasped in his lap.

"I think he was a kind of writer."

"When was the war of the American Revolution fought?"

"In 1812, I think; I'm not quite sure."

The newspapers thought this was very funny. One published a cartoon of Ford standing in a corner with a dunce cap on his head. The picture offended him. He does not mind jokes about his car but he resents those that concern him personally. He fears extremes and puts his trust in action at all times. He does not smoke or drink, sleeps six and a half hours out of twenty-four, and eats meagerly. He never lets an obligation to be cordial interfere with his routine. There was in Dearborn, for instance, a man named Coffin who had been a sheriff and lost his job through the influence of a politician Ford disliked. To show his sympathy Ford gave Coffin the restaurant concession at one of his plants and started him in business. Naturally, Coffin was grateful. When he got word that Ford was coming to lunch in his restaurant he kept his chef up late making a cake and bought two turkeys and dressed the table as if it were Thanksgiving, as, in a way, it was. Sitting down to lunch, Ford looked at the bird smoking on the table, the colored candles and elaborate cake. He said, "I think I'd like some milk and crackers."

That he has behaved like this a good many times is partly because he and his family don't care much for parties. With the stiff pride of a country aristocracy, they have kept close relationships only with a few of the old farmer people near Dearborn—Horzens, Wards, Woodworths, Schovens. Every year at Christmas they give a party in their big stone house; the rest of the time there is not much entertainment. Sometimes when a guest comes, Edsel Ford, to oblige his father, puts a record on the phonograph (a present from Mr. Edison) and plays an accompaniment on the drum. With his knee thrown over the arm of a chair and his foot swinging, Ford listens, smiling with one side of his face. In the winter logs burn in the stone fireplace over which is the motto, "Chop your own wood and it will warm you twice."

When there is no one to entertain he will sit down at the player piano or the automatic organ or stroll out to the workshop he has fitted out in a detached building. When he is there the servants say to callers, "Mr. Ford is not at home. . . ." He is suspicious of strangers and has made it hard for anyone to approach him. One of his offices at the plant is at the top of a steep flight of iron stairs. People coming to see him always arrive a little out of breath, and this in some peculiar fashion seems to gratify him. He has thought nothing of keeping famous callers waiting for hours. Three representatives of the government of Mexico, coming to place a big order at his plant, waited for him from two in the afternoon till seven in the evening. When Theodore Roosevelt visited Detroit Ford invited him to come to the plant at eleven in the morning. Roosevelt was late. Ford went on with his work in other parts of the factory, calling his secretary every few minutes to ask if the ex-President had come.

"No, sir," said the secretary at twelve o'clock.

Ford said: "Well, if he's not here by twelve-thirty you tell him I've gone fishing."

Over and over he has demonstrated this peculiar pride—"proud as a king," journalists call him. A king leaves home to visit the meanest of his border towns. Ford entrenched in his vast but provincial domain is as proud as a farmer. With the land hunger seen in most farmers' sons who have grown rich, he has bought more than ten thousand acres outside Dearborn and cultivates them at a profit. He likes to line up half a dozen motor reapers at the edge of a wheatfield and see them all start together.

Sitting on a fence he watches the blond wheat tops shiver and fall sideways.

"Say," he remarked to a friend who had come down for this review, "you wouldn't think that food could look so slick, would you?"

Just as he thinks of standing wheat as food he thinks of money for what it will do. He never tried hard to be rich—he says he has "been too busy making cars"—yet an inherited parsimony makes him close-fisted. He lost the senatorial election in Michigan chiefly because he would not spend money enough campaigning. But though he watches his billion-dollar accounts as closely as a housewife watches her cracked teapot he has no reverence for the tangibility of coin: When he goes on a trip he sometimes carries ten thousand dollars in his pocket and at other times he has to ask his aides for a twenty-dollar bill. Once his treasurer complained that he had not received a check for a hundred and twenty thousand dollars due from another company as deposit for an order of Ford cars. Telegrams went back and forth. At last the check was found. Ford had it. A servant had taken it out of the pocket of a suit he had sent to be pressed.

Both his absent-mindedness and his way of nursing grudges are habits typical of lonely men. Ford has always kept to himself. Not many people in Detroit have ever seen him. He belongs to several dignified clubs which have kept his name on their books for years—sometimes with a complimentary membership or because Edsel or Mrs. Ford paid the dues—but the only one he ever goes to is not recognized by the Social Register: the Dearborn Country Club. Once or twice a year his wife used to take him to the benefit shows of the Detroit Players' Club. He would come in late and arrange his party so as to have a friend on each side of him and two behind. If in spite of these precautions someone came over to speak to him he would rear his head back on his long neck with an air that indicated that if he wanted audiences he would solicit them. He has stopped going to the Players' Club.

Once he took up golf. A pro named Robertson was engaged by the Dearborn Club to be Ford's private instructor, the members heard. In fact, the manufacturer was twice seen on the course without his coat but wearing his usual high stand-up collar. Then Robertson left, and Ford quit playing. Nobody ever found out his score.

City people's clubs and parties, city people's sports —it is not likely they could ever interest him. Thin, wiry, and with an awkward grace in everything, he still gets up before seven; he likes to walk over his land, vaulting the stone fences. In the city he wears a gray felt hat and in the country no hat at all. He is a good skater and clever at the old-fashioned dances he tried to revive two years ago for the instruction of a jazzing generation. His favorite musical instrument is a violin, and his favorite author is John Burroughs. He used to whittle cedar shingles into ingenious toys for Edsel, now a man in his thirties, with an alert face, a calm manner, and bright ties. Henry Ford believes that his son had an important share in designing the new car. "We have a good man in Edsel," he said to an associate; "he knows what an automobile ought to look like."

Edsel and plump, dark-eyed Mrs. Henry Ford, whom Ford calls "Mother" and speaks of as "The Believer" because he says she has always had more faith in his ideas than he had himself, are probably the only two human beings whose existence makes any serious difference to him. In the old days he was less alone, but as he has grown older he has quarreled with more and more of his old friends, until now, at sixty-seven, he distrusts friendship as a general proposition.

"I must never allow myself to become so intimate with anyone again," he said after quarreling with an associate he had known all his life.

Horace and John Dodge, Alexander Malcolmson,

James Couzens, Norval Hawkins—these and many more who have been associated with him in his work for one reason or another left him.

It may be foolish to criticize a man for losing his friends, yet many people dislike Ford more for this than anything else; they look suspiciously at all he has done, knowing that when anyone complains of his friends it is a sign that life has failed to please him. The easy explanation is, of course, that his success has victimized him, left him lonely, but that is not a real solution either—he has been lonely all his life. Perhaps, chilled with the cold of some interior winter, he lacks a quality common to less urgent men—nothing as vague as "warmth" or the "instinct to enjoy" but a quality without a name, powerful and evasive. He seems to be wondering himself what it is he lacks. He is more restless than he used to be, thinner; in the last few years he has developed an odd gesture—putting both hands against his cheek bones he pulls his fingers slowly down his cheeks. At such a moment more than ever there seems to be some birdlike spirit in his face, listening and watching, wary and light.

II

Henry Ford's story makes him seem a great and simple man who has given his whole life to the service of a practical idea. His public activities, with their mixture of petty malice and grandiose idealism, make him seem mildly unbalanced. Between these two points of view are many anecdotes which show that he is neither heroic nor unbalanced, but very shrewd and well able to think things out for himself.

For example, take the scheme he used for getting money when he was hard up after the war. An editor in Battle Creek had spread the news that the Ford Company was going to close its doors and that Henry Ford was passing round his hat in Wall Street. This was not true, but it was true that few people were buying automobiles, that Ford had ninety-three thousand of them on hand, that in December, 1920, with twenty million dollars in cash, he had to make payments of fifty-eight million. One New York banker went to Dearborn and without an appointment called on Ford and offered to lend him as much money as he wanted at a high rate of interest. "I don't need it," Ford kept repeating; "I've got all I want."

He had thought out a plan. Instead of stopping production he made it go faster. He estimated how many cars his dealers could sell if times were good and then he notified them to buy exactly that number. "Your quota will be . . ." the form letter ran.

Twenty per cent of the price of each car was to be paid right away, the rest on delivery. Implicit in the letter was a warning that if an agent disobeyed orders Ford would take the agency away from him. In most towns the right to sell Ford cars and parts is more valuable than any other automobile concession. The dealers knew what it was worth. All over the country mechanics and garage men borrowed from their banks and their friends and mortgaged houses to send Ford the money he needed.

He showed his satisfaction in a characteristic way. He put ten million dollars in gold into the vaults of a bank in Dearborn and invited to lunch the banker who had offered to finance him. After a silent meal at which the banker ate partridge and the manufacturer sipped milk, Ford is said to have taken his guest down to the vaults and indicating the piles of bullion said:

"Now, sir, if you think that you can break me, step inside."

Whether or not this actually took place does not matter much; even the fact that it has been told so often shows something about Ford's character. He has a talent for getting publicity out of everything he does. An instance is the way he helped the birds in Louisiana. He had heard that a bill for bird conservation was pending in the state legislature and

wrote to a friend in Louisiana asking what chance
it had of being passed. Hearing that it needed help,
he began to issue stories about birds to the newspapers. They were little stories, fifty or a hundred
words long, each with an interesting fact in it—
how one kind of bird ate the worms that killed
crops, how another, flying, dropped from its mouth
the seeds that started forests. That Louisiana had a
bill to save birds gave a news lead to these stories.
Every one of them had Ford's name in it. They appeared for several months. The bill was passed, and
Ford, in helping to pass it, had got several hundred
thousand dollars' worth of advertising.

It would be ridiculous to say that he helped the
birds for the sake of publicity. He likes birds and
knows a lot about them. It would be equally ridiculous to say that he did not foresee what a good thing
it would be for him to back the bill. He foresees
the consequences of everything he does, often with
great subtlety. On Armistice Day he was having
lunch at the Dearborn plant. Through the window
he could see several hundred workmen putting up a
factory that had been planned for war work. One of
the plant superintendents, lunching with him, said:
"I'll have to stop work on that to-morrow, Mr.
Ford. Every minute they spend there is costing you
money. We can never use the building now."

Ford said :"Don't stop. Let them keep on slowly, and when things get more settled pull it down. If you throw all those men out of work at a time like this you will discourage everybody."

When he draws a bad conclusion it is usually because he has not had enough facts to work with. The mistake he has regretted more than any other was his attack on the Jews, and one cause for his regret was that he did not properly estimate the effect of the attack on his political and economic position.

What gave him the idea in the first place is hard to guess. It may have been because a Jewess, Rosika Schwimmer, persuaded him to make his Peace Trip, an expedition that left him feeling that he had been somehow fooled. It may have been because he grew up in a country district where there were no Jews and where the farmers, like all religious and uneducated people, thought of the Hebrew race with a physical revulsion borrowed in some confused way from their Bibles. A few small encounters of his own had something to do with it. Once he called at a New York bank to cash a draft forwarded to him from Europe. At the teller's window he was told to go upstairs, "and when I got up there," he said afterward, "I found a lot of Jews sitting around smoking cigars as long as that chimney." They held up his draft on a technicality. For some time afterward he spoke angrily of the experience, pointing out the cigar smokers as exceptional examples of racial nastiness, but later he began to say the Jews were all alike. The idea of attacking them formed in his mind until it suddenly took shape alongside a political idea —his old ambition to be president.

Henry Ford has always wanted and perhaps still wants to be president. He wanted the senatorship in his own state as one step toward the White House, and when he lost the election he was far from apathetic concerning the impeachment proceedings against his successful opponent, Truman Newberry.

A cub reporter drafted the views which Ford presented to the people of this country as an inducement for electing him their chief executive. He had met this reporter on the street and taken a liking to him because he "looked like a good mechanic." When he asked what he could do for him the reporter said: "Let me publish your platform, Mr. Ford."

Ford said: "Well, son, I haven't got a platform written. But I tell you what you do. You know as much about my views as anyone else—you go ahead and write the platform, and when you get it written I'll sign it."

He had visited the White House several times— once to talk to President Wilson about his proposed Peace Trip. During the interview, with his leg over

a chair, he told the Ford joke he made up himself
—the one about the man who had his grave made
big enough to hold his car, saying, "My Ford got
me out of every hole so far and I guess she'll get me
out of that one." In reply President Wilson recited
the limerick about a lady who rode on a tiger. As he
left, Ford turned around in the limousine that was
taking him down the drive and looking back at the
White House said with his one-sided smile: "It
seems right comfortable."

Through every discouragement he never lost hope
that some day he might get a nomination—from
which party he didn't care. By attacking the Jews
he may have seen a way to revive his candidacy.

His reasoning might have been something like
this: the population of the United States was only
three per cent Jewish, wasn't it? The Gentiles didn't
like the Jews, did they? All right, if anyone attacked
the Jews, wouldn't the majority of the population
vote for him? He launched his propaganda with
characteristic efficiency, working with the help of
well known anti-Jewish fanatics. He hired a scholar
to translate the Talmud in such a way as to make it
derogatory to the Jews whenever possible. He did
not stop his propaganda until his advisers convinced
him that no candidate who failed to carry either
New York or Ohio could be president and that no

one could carry New York or Ohio who was offensive to the Jews.

At about this time, too, Ford saw his sales drop sharply in the East and Middle West. He has always believed that he would lose possible votes wherever he loses sales.

Through the autumn of 1923 his political followers waited in suspense. December 12th had been designated to all agents and adherents as Decision Day. On this day he had promised to tell the Ford-for-President clubs (organized in Detroit at his expense) whether he would run in 1924. A little while before that day he had an interview with President Coolidge. Neither he nor the President would repeat what they said to each other, but at twelve-thirty on the morning of Decision Day Ford called the newspaper men around him and announced that he did not want to be president.

If his dislike for Rosika Schwimmer was one element in Ford's attack on the Jews he cannot like her any better now. His chief grudge against her, however, is the one he bears her for seducing him into the Peace Trip. Feeling that he had been made ridiculous, he never forgave anyone connected with that expedition.

Rosika Schwimmer was a dark-eyed Hungarian Jewess with resonant voice and energetic gestures.

She went to Detroit in 1916 bringing letters from the great ministers of countries that were at war —letters in which men like Viscount Grey and Bethmann-Hollweg said they were tired of fighting and ready to arbitrate if anyone invited them to. Rosika Schwimmer carried the letters in a green brief case which she tied to her body when she went to sleep.

Henry Ford did not at once agree to finance the expedition she proposed. It was not until President Wilson refused to give it any official support that he got angry and said he would put it over alone. That night he called up his wife from Washington. Their conversation has been reported in various ways. The generally accepted version is this:

FORD: Hello, Mother, how are you?

MRS. FORD: I'm all right. What did you decide?

FORD: I decided you and I are going on a little trip.

MRS. FORD: Where?

FORD: We're going to Europe. We're going to take some people with us.

MRS. FORD: Oh, no, we're not.

Even William Jennings Bryan refused to go. As the whistle blew Ford stood at the head of the gangplank with Thomas Edison. Edison said: "Goodbye, old man." He put out his hand. Ford took it and held it; he said: "Are you going to stay on board?" Edison shook his head. Ford kept hold of his hand. "You must stay on board," he said. "You must stay on board and go with me." Edison was the last man to go ashore.

In a long black coat with a fur collar, bareheaded, with the tight smile of a sick man, Ford looked down at the noisy crowd on the pier. He had caught cold the day before and was sick for the rest of the trip. Everything went wrong. The papers said that he had chartered the *Oscar II;* this was not true. He had talked at first about chartering it but decided not to because of the expense; instead he paid the passages of his delegates and put three or four in each cabin. There was trouble about his letter of credit —it was made out for ten days, and he had to send home for more money. Worst of all, the newspaper men sent out stories over the ship's wireless making fun of the whole expedition.

The captain intercepted some of the messages. "Are you going to let them send this stuff?" he asked Ford.

"The boys are my guests," Ford said. "Let them say anything they want."

Toward Christiania through the winter seas went the small ugly boat, instrument of a parable. Horror and frozen wounds, all the bewilderment of a war in which death issued from machines, to be ended and peace restored by this picnic of school teachers, adventurers, publicity men. In an overheated cabin littered with pamphlets Henry Ford nursed his cold. He had a fever and talked only in whispers.

Now for the first time he must have begun to suspect his judgment of events and to wonder whether the voices of his advisers had not drowned in his ears the whisper of good luck that he had followed all his life.

Weak and white, he came on deck at Christiania to see a crowd of blue-eyed people waving flags on the wharf. Tears jumped to his eyes, and leaning over the railing he waved back at them. Some of his hope had revived, and when the reporters came to him he gave out a statement in his threadlike voice. "Tell the citizens of Christiania I will not leave their city till I have looked them in the face and thanked them in person for this welcome."

But his hope left him, and a few days later he stole out of the city at three o'clock in the morning.

He felt then that Rosika Schwimmer's letters meant nothing; the fighting countries would not talk of peace. The night his party went on to Stockholm he hid in another part of the station, waiting for a train that would take him south.

In the course of time, on the boat coming home, he got back strength enough to pretend that he was satisfied.

"The war is still going on, Mr. Ford," a reporter reminded him. He saw that the manufacturer did not want to talk about his trip.

"I know," Ford said quickly. "We failed there, but I got some valuable information, all the same."

"What was that?"

"I found out that Russia is going to be a great market for tractors."

While the Ford company was still turning out Model T it was said that if any employee made a suggestion for improving the car he was apt to be discharged. I don't believe that, but it is true that Ford likes to suggest his own ideas—he needs subordinates but cannot tolerate partners.

In odd places, with the shrewdness of a horse-dealer, he has picked the men who serve him now. His secretary, Liebold, was a caddy at the Dearborn Country Club. Ford liked his smooth Scandinavian face, his energetic, thoughtful subservience. Another of his executives had served a term in Jackson. Getting out, he had started in business for himself as an accountant and his friends liked his nerve so well that they put his name up for the Detroit Club. He was blackballed. Ford heard about it. He said: "Well, if he isn't good enough for the Detroit Club, maybe he's good enough for me."

Years afterwards this man who had become a millionaire and an important figure in the automobile industry quarreled with Ford and left. Nearly all his first associates have left him. John Dodge and his quiet brother Horace left. They shook hands with Ford again at Edsel's wedding, but the next day they sued for their share of twenty-nine million dollars which they claimed he had withheld from their share of the company profits. He sometimes speaks of this day as the saddest of his life. He has never been able to understand how the Dodges could have come to the wedding when they were planning to sue.

In spite of his hurt sentiments he had to pay them most of the money they sued for.

Alexander Malcomson, a Detroit coal and lumber dealer and an original investor in the Ford company, had put his smart young clerk, James Couzens, into the business to watch his money. Couzens had become one of Ford's most important executives. After years of association he objected to some propaganda that was coming out in the *Dearborn Independent*.

"If that stays in, I quit," he said suddenly.

"It stays in," Ford said.

He was angry with Couzens for spending too much time away from the plant and for arrogating authority which he felt belonged only to him, Ford. "He cost me fifty cents on every car I made," he said of Couzens.

Quarrels of this sort, duplicated in many instances, make his officials say: "If you are a friend of Ford's don't work for him."

Some will tell you that his fights all start because he insists on finding out everything that goes on in the plant and its related businesses. One dealer who had made big profits from the sale of Ford cars got a letter from the sales department telling him what sort of glass to use in the windows of his new garage. Another young man who had married a rich wife got the Ford agency in a busy town. Making money, he took life easy for a while. Then suddenly his habits changed. He began getting down to work at nine o'clock.

"By God, I was scared," he explained to a friend; "I got a telegram from Henry Ford telling me if I didn't get down to work on time he'd fire me."

Ford has a "personal information" department through which he keeps tabs on what goes on. Stories are told to show that he has used this department to satisfy small animosities. A boy who had leased a red gas station near the Dearborn plant refused to sell Ford's benzol because his customers said it was bad. Ford's secret service found a·joker in his lease which provided that he rented the land on which the gas station stood but not the land between the station and the road. Ford had a fence built keeping cars from driving up to the station.

"It looked," said the judge awarding the agent a decision in his suit for damages, "like the fence an old woman builds when she is mad with her neighbor."

He does not answer his own mail nor did he write "Mr. Ford's Page" in the *Dearborn Independent*, but he gives a surprising amount of time to petty contests of just this kind. Other incidents have also made him seem petty, yet his grudges are nearly balanced by his sudden kindnesses. He likes to befriend those who have no right to expect anything. Men with prison records can usually get jobs in his plant; he employs more tubercular and crippled workmen than any other manufacturer in the world, believing that a sick man can do routine work as well as a whole one and that work cures most ailments.

He was one of the first industrialists to give his men an eight-hour day—this, and his announcement in 1914 that five dollars a day would be the minimum wage in his plant, are generally pointed out as his greatest benevolences. As a matter of fact, he had found by experiment that most workers could not keep going efficiently for more than eight hours, and his high wage-scale became the greatest advertisement ever written for the Ford car.

Though the provisions that concern his business are dictated more by hard sense than by benevolence, and though he says that charity is "degrading to both parties," he is capable in his personal relationships of graceful, unexpected courtesies. When John Burroughs attacked automobiles, saying that to own one kept a person from enjoying nature, Ford sent him a car with his compliments and a letter saying, "This will give you a chance to test your statement." The naturalist took back what he had said, and he and Ford became friends.

When these two, with Edison and Harvey Firestone, who makes tires for Ford cars, took their summer trips into the woods, Ford always did the cooking. He made what he called brigand steaks, cutting the meat into strips and broiling it with bacon. Edison would take naps through the day and read most of the night, rigging up a reading light out of an automobile battery. He and Ford have known each other since both were fairly young.

Ford was still trying to construct a car when he made a special trip to Atlantic City to hear Edison lecture. Afterward he spoke to the inventor in a corner of the room, telling him his ideas for perfecting the gas engine, and Edison encouraged him. "I hope you get what you are after," he said to young Ford, who must have looked then much as he does now, perhaps more awkward and stronger, with baggy clothes and strained, attentive eyes. At five o'clock on a rainy morning in April, 1893, he finished his first car. His wife had been sitting up all night, and she came out on the porch to watch him crank it and drive off. After running a few yards the engine choked and stopped. Ford pushed it into the yard and went upstairs to bed. He had finished the first move toward the hope that Edison had expressed for him. Naturally, now that the hope is realized, he is most at ease with men like the inventor and Firestone because they belong to his own tradition, reminding him of a part of his own career that was hard-pressed and unconfused, a long and difficult time, a great story.

Many writers have been attracted to the story of Ford's rise, seeing in it a chance for a certain artistic effect—the background of the farm, the country school, with later on a young mechanic bent over his bench in a mid-Western city. They have crusted his boyhood with many anecdotes which may be true but tell nothing about him. Almost any country boy has tried at some time to fix farm

machinery or take a watch apart. Henry Ford was
not a prodigy. He was lanky, awkward, clever, and
shy; he had a bad memory and disliked cows. The
difference between him and any other boy who
might get interested in mechanics was that Ford
wanted a practical answer to everything. Farm work
made him feel sick, but he didn't like reading either.
Patient and shrewd when working with material
things, he could fix a watch when he was thirteen;
he stopped selling Scarborough's maps and Grant's
Memoirs and for pocket money went round the
neighborhood fixing clocks and watches. In 1880,
when he was seventeen, he got a job with the Dry-
dock Power Company of Detroit.

How he lived during the next eight years—earning at first two dollars and a half a week, working
at night fixing watches, later experimenting for
himself—is part of the legend already printed in
schoolbooks. For no definite purpose, except to learn
about machines, he suffered a good many privations,
and from his letters his parents detected that he
was getting tired of the city. His father offered him
certain acres of standing timber if he would come
home. Henry Ford accepted. He saw that the offer
would give him a chance to get married.

That winter he courted Clara Bryant, a farmer's
daughter, plump and dark. He drove her in a red

sleigh to dances in big Michigan barns where the fiddlers, sitting up on carriage seats, played "Money Musk" and "Turkey in the Straw," and each girl brought a layer cake which her sweetheart bought at auction.

Ford has restored in every detail the square clapboard farmhouse in which he grew up. He remembered that the trees were stunted. When the new trees he planted grew too fast he had tree surgeons stunt them with wires. But at the time of his marriage the trees and the house could not hold him; he took his wife to a lodging house in Bagley Avenue, Detroit, and got a night job in the Detroit Electric Company. In his workshop on the farm he had been experimenting with a gasoline motor, and he took his model to Detroit and put it in a disused shop in State Street. Going into the Electric Company was part of a definite scheme. He wanted to study ignition. The study of engines, at first just something to do, then a means of getting away from the farm, had turned into a single and passionate idea which filled his mind and yanked his whole life after it.

One thing ought to be made clear—he did not invent the motor car or any important part of it. A man named Selden, to whom the first automobile makers paid large royalties, had a patent on a "road-coach propelled by gasoline" which included also a way of making the vehicle go faster or slower by shifting gears; later Ford contested and defeated Selden's patent on the ground that Selden had not made an automobile that was practical. But at the beginning he did not bother about patents. The car he made in his workshop out of bicycle wheels, a buggy body, and two four-horsepower cylinders set over the rear axle, was a combination of many existing ideas.

Owning a car gave him a reputation in Detroit. Since several people sued him for scaring their horses he asked the mayor for a permit to drive his buggy-car—the first motor license issued in America. When he left the car outside a shop he would chain it to a lamp-post to keep small boys from snitching it. News of his antics came to the offices of the Detroit Electric Company. One day the president called him into his office and told him that if he stopped fooling with his wagon the company would make him general superintendent and raise his pay to one hundred and fifty dollars a month—and that if he wouldn't he could get out.

This moment was an important one in Ford's life. He had saved a little money; the only thing he could do was to leave the electric company and try to make a living out of the machine he had spent so long perfecting.

By this time quite a few gasoline cars had been built and sold in the Middle West. He found a group of Detroit business men who were willing to risk some money backing him. They organized the Detroit Automobile Company with a capital of fifty thousand dollars, ten thousand of which had been paid in. He was chief engineer at a hundred dollars a month.

For three years the Detroit Automobile Company turned out cars; the policy of the directors was to make a few cars to order and sell them for high prices. This was contrary to everything Ford believed. He kept insisting that cars should be made wholesale and sold cheap to everyone. As soon as he could he left the company, which the Lelands afterward reorganized as the Cadillac Company.

Everyone in those days was talking about racing cars. Alexander Winton with his famous car, the *Bullet,* was track champion of the United States. Ford worked for nine months in his little shop making a fast two-cylinder engine which he fitted on a skeleton chassis. In 1902 he challenged Winton to a race. His own account contains the facts: "We met at Grosse Pointe track. I beat him."

The race gave Ford a lot of advertising but did not attract any backers. Tom Cooper, a bicycle rider, lent him money enough to build another racer, planning to bet on him and clean up at Grosse Pointe the next spring. Ford built a big red car that went so fast nobody dared drive it. It was named *999* after a famous engine of the Empire State Express. When it was driven fast, flames jumped out of the roaring motor. There was only one seat. Cooper, trying to find someone who would drive it, finally thought of a man who was not afraid of anything—a bicycle rider he had raced against in Salt Lake City and whose name was Barney Oldfield.

Answering "sure" to the telegram they sent him, Oldfield went to Detroit, learned to drive in a week, and beat his nearest rival by half a mile in the three-mile race at Grosse Pointe. A week later the Ford Motor Company was organized.

Alexander Malcolmson was the biggest investor, with seven thousand dollars, and a man named John Gray next, with three thousand. John Anderson and Horace Rackham, two young lawyers, were given a thousand dollars' worth of stock apiece for incorporating the company. Vernon Fry, Charles Bennet, Albert Strelow were other original investors in that fabulous little company, incorporated for a hundred thousand dollars, of which twenty-eight thousand was subscribed—the only sum the company ever received from any source but operation. Later Ford bought out some of the thousand-dollar stockholders at prices ranging from seven and a half million to ten million dollars.

From the day in June, 1903, when the first Ford car was sold, business went fast. Henry Ford himself, in goggles and a round fur cap, drove 999 over a cinder track laid on the ice at Lake St. Claire, breaking the world's record for a mile with a time of thirty-nine seconds and a fraction. After that sales went faster than ever. The factory in Mack Avenue got too small, and a larger place was rented on Piquette Street, and in 1910 at Highland Park. In 1908 Ford was making a hundred cars a day and selling them for six hundred dollars apiece. He had introduced what he called progressive assembling, an idea borrowed from the Chicago slaughter houses where he had seen the carcasses of animals hung on a continuously moving conveyor and passing down a line of butchers who cut the particular parts assigned to them. He started to haul a chassis through his shop with a rope and windlass. As it moved on the chassis grew. By 1916 he had made over a million cars, over four million by 1921.

In 1922 he bought the Lincoln Motor Company at auction, put Edsel in control of it, introduced his own manufacturing methods. In the Lincoln plant, as in the Ford plants at Highland Park and Fordson, everything moves by belts and chains. Big conveyors are fed by little conveyors. A man who loafs is hopelessly swamped, yet everything works without hurry, wastelessly. When Ford was making the old model it took him thirty hours to convert raw iron ore into an automobile and deliver it to a purchaser three hundred miles away. He expects to reach the same efficiency with Model A by the end of this year.

In spite of the new ideas, drawn from things outside his business, which have mixed him up and made him make mistakes, the story of Ford's life still shows him as he is—the farmer's son turned mechanic, shrewd, patient, suspicious, and calculating, putting his trust in action, and driven on without rest by a single idea which has lifted him from need to a position of titanic power.

Richer than any king alive, with time now to stretch himself, Ford, the Titan, pushed out his power round him in many directions.

He started the *Dearborn Independent*. He wanted a stick to shake at writers who attacked him. Not knowing much about the writing business he began slowly. He bought for five thousand dollars an old web press which the *American Boy* magazine had discarded, hired a pressman named Louie Bunker,

and assembled a staff—Pipp of the Detroit *Times,*
Cameron, Rowland. He sent a representative to a
magazine writer.

"Mr. Ford is starting a magazine. He wants it to
be the best in America. He thought you might suggest some ideas."

"Certainly," the magazine man said. "If he wants
to have the best magazine tell him to get the best
writers. Tell him to get Shaw, Kipling, Galsworthy
—people like that. For thirty thousand an issue he
can have the best magazine in the world."

Hearing this, Ford shook his head.

"That's foolish," he said; "this is going to be a
national magazine, isn't it? Well, how did this Shaw
and Galsworthy get their reputations, eh? Writing
for national magazines, didn't they? All right, if you
write my magazine, won't you have reputations like
them? All right. Go ahead and write it."

When the potential Shaws and Galsworthys had
got out a few issues Ford gave another illustration
of how his ideas on all subjects are reflected from
automobile production. Calling in the editor he complained of the way the paper was run. He had noticed
that each article was being written by a separate
man—one wrote funny stories, another editorials,
another the stories that had facts in them. That
wasn't efficient. If a magazine was made up of

articles, then the article was the unit of production.
One mechanic didn't make a car all by himself. An
article should be passed along the line of production
—one worker could put in the humor, another the
facts, another the moral. Only when the editor, using
images Ford could understand, explained that
the magazine, not the article, was the unit of production—that the magazine passed along a production line while one mechanic put in humor, another
thought, another facts—did the manufacturer nod,
smile, exclaim, "I see, I see. Well, maybe. Go ahead."

The *Dearborn Independent* was hard to sell, but
Ford found a way to sell it. He forced it on his
dealers and made them distribute it among their customers. In this way it reached a lead-pipe circulation
of seven hundred thousand. Before it was discon-
tinued, in December 1927, he had made it run without much help. He ceased making his agents buy it.
Most of the newspaper men who wrote for it seemed
ashamed to have their names in Mr. Ford's paper.
They explained quickly that they could sell him stuff
nobody else would buy.

He is said to have lost five hundred thousand dollars a year on the *Dearborn Independent,* but he was
satisfied. He had a medium through which to boost
his political hopes and fight back at his critics. He
had not at that time forgotten how a jury of his

peers decided that the Chicago *Tribune,* in calling him an anarchist, had damaged him to the extent of six cents.

Before he had stopped worrying about his newspaper he bought a hospital. It had been a public organization that depended on charity for support. It had run into debt and the Detroit *Times* had started a campaign for funds. Ford's name was published as one of the patrons of the failing hospital. His wife showed him the story.

"I see that you are a failure financially," she said.

He repeats this with a smile, saying: "I decided to give the contributors their money back and run the place myself."

Because he thinks that Americans "ought to resent pampering" he runs the hospital for a profit, but a workman can go there to have his arm set, and the workman's wife to have her baby at reasonable cost. When a patient goes to the hospital for any treatment his whole body is examined and card-indexed. Another rule forbids the doctors who practise there to practise anywhere else. The nurses punch time-clocks. The charges are four dollars and a half a day, one hundred and twenty-five dollars for a major operation. Surgeons have called it the most efficient hospital in the world.

Soon after it was organized, Ford went into the

airplane business. An airplane engineer named Stout had asked him to buy stock in a company that he was starting in Detroit. Ford refused, but said he would give the land for the airport gratis. When planes began to drone over Dearborn his curiosity in anything mechanical made him spend considerable time at the airport. He would lean in the doorways of hangars talking to the mechanics. Pretty soon he bought out the investors and took the whole thing over.

He bought the Wayside Inn. The consciousness of his own importance as an American character that has made him preserve the house he was born in and every souvenir of his early work, had sharpened his interest in a story that this old place at Sudbury, Massachusetts, where Longfellow wrote the "Tales of a Wayside Inn," was falling down for want of money to repair it. He renovated it with characteristic thoroughness. Now visitors are welcomed by hostesses who show them upstairs to deep Colonial beds, while waitresses set pans of biscuits to rise by the open fire. On the walls are hayrakes, posting horns, flipping irons, tankards, spurs, warming pans, and a maple-sugar bucket inscribed with the names of Harvey Firestone and the Prince of Wales. Ford's imagination went farther. He decided to have a whole primitive American community, with grist mills and a wool-carding factory, as background for the Little Red Schoolhouse a few miles off, which he bought too, hearing that it was the place referred to in the rhyme about Mary and her Little Lamb.

The people of Sudbury, to whom these changes have brought a lot of money, could see the advantage of restoring landmarks but could not understand why he insisted on having the beams chopped by hand, put together with wooden pegs, and dragged to their places by oxen with brass-tipped horns. Would he admit visitors who drove up in automobiles, they asked.

His interest in antiques, his associates said, was the only thing that could have made him buy the Detroit, Toledo & Ironton Railroad—it had been losing money for years, but Ford made it a model of efficiency that has been copied all over the world. His freight cars never have hot boxes because he invented a lubricating system like an automobile's for their wheels. He bought a line of steamboats to bring metal ore down from his mines. He pays the crews twice as much as other boat owners but forbids them to smoke. Coal comes to him from his own mines in West Virginia and Kentucky. He converts a ton worth five dollars into coke and by-products worth twelve dollars and a half. He decided to make his own windshields, and in doing so became the second largest glass maker in the world. After experimenting for three years his plant began to turn out plate glass in continuous sheets, a thing experts said could never be done.

He tried to buy Muscle Shoals. He planned to use the electric power drawn from water to start industries of many sorts that would in turn cause new towns and even cities to be built along the rocky shallow of the Tennessee River where the government had built a dam and a nitrate plant and then abandoned them. He is still interested in Muscle Shoals, but this and all his side projects—even his ambition to be President—matter very little compared to his interest in making cars.

When he built his first car he probably knew more about gasoline engines than anyone else in the world. There are only three or four men now who know as much as he does, and they are engineers rather than manufacturers. Most of the companies now trying in a fierce trade war to get their prices down to his have adopted his methods of production. Ford likes to be copied—he keeps no secrets. Any technical expert can go through the plant at Fordson and stay as long as he likes. The officials who take him round will answer all his questions and even give him blueprints to take home. The difficulty of under-selling Ford is not a matter of method but of performance.

Long ago, in his own machine shop, Ford worked by trial and error. He made a part and then tested it. In making the new car, Model A, he worked the same way. He organized two departments—one to design, the other to test. He provided no way for these separate organizations to report to each other. The designers would make a gear—the testers would send it back with the teeth ripped out. The stripped gear was the statement of what had happened. The designers only knew they had been successful when a part did not come back.

Some newspapers reported that he had spent one hundred million dollars making Model A. This is not true. He spent perhaps fifteen to twenty million dollars—very little considering the scale he works on. By the end of the year he was making ten thousand cars a day and employing a hundred and fifty thousand men. For a while he lost money on every car, but he insisted on having the model fully equipped with accessories. When his testing and designing staffs had set up a few cars he got into a sedan and drove it over stones and planks in a lot behind the Fordson plant, sending it back with a criticism written in crayon on a piece of yellow paper: "Good, but it rides too hard. Put on hydraulic shock absorbers."

Silver-haired now and a billionaire, looking twenty years older than he did ten years ago, he is still anxiously concerned with practical mechanics. It is still as hard as ever for anyone who does not know him to relate his brilliant practical intelligence to some of the wild things he has done and some of the statements, positive and scarcely sound, that he has worded with such admirable terseness. It is not likely that Ford himself would defend all the ideas he has had in the last ten years. Some of them—like this scheme for building factories out in the wheat fields so that when farmers were not tending crops they could be making shoes or carburetors—were harmless but not reasoned out; others, like the attack on the Jews, seemed, to liberal-minded people, to have been produced by a machine capable of manufacturing notions but incapable of reasoning.

In a way, Ford's mind is such a machine. One of his friends told me he thought Ford kept always before him, as an example of what he wanted to be like, the image of a dollar watch. That may be more than a fancy. Ford fixed enough watches when he was a boy to recognize the poetry of the symbol, wasteless and symmetrical. But that figure too leaves out a lot of qualities that belong to Ford; perhaps the only true criticism you can make of him is that he lacks something that has been a part of most authentically great men and which may be called the General Idea. He has fixed his mind too hard on one detail after another to understand the proper relationship of all things. It is the lack of this idea that makes him seem bleak and erratic when he is only puzzled. To that lack also may be due the listening, guessing quality of his face.

But always his own character survives the imagery concocted to explain it. Provincial and isolated, he is a great man in spite of his sharp angles, perhaps even because of them, and because he represents so many other Americans who are just like him. There are thousands of farmers in Michigan and Ohio who express thoughts like his in almost identical language and who lack only his power of turning them into facts. There are mechanics running red gas stations in country towns who lack the brains and courage to invent anything but who have his kind of a wiry, meager body and conjecturing mind, and who tinker with machines all day just as he used to. Ford represents all these men, and he represents something more abstract. Progress, the Iron Age—no matter what you call it, he has had an important part in its development. And so you come down to his real significance, which might be put in this way: if it were possible to preserve alive, for the interests of history, one man from each century and country—not, of course, the best or wisest, but the one who represented most thoroughly the hopes, crudities, background, and achievements of his place—no one could better represent this time and the United States than Henry Ford.

PORTRAIT OF A DUTCHMAN

PORTRAIT OF A DUTCHMAN

WALTER HAGEN weighs about a hundred and eighty pounds. His eyes look small and pale in the sunburned folds of his face. His hands thicken into muscular wrists, and his chin (which retreats as if, in a setback position, it formed a stronger prop for the other bones of his skull) gives attraction to his face by preventing it from being handsome. He smiles continually, smokes cigarettes, and dresses in light-colored clothes. He is the greatest golf player in the world.

The last assertion must seem a little strident. I am willing to let it seem so because it does not represent a personal opinion, but a conclusion dictated by records and by arithmetic. Hagen has been playing tournament golf since 1914. In this period he has won the American Open twice, the British Open four times, the Metropolitan Open three times, the Western Open three times, the French Open once, the North and South Open four times, the West Coast Open four times, and the Professional Golfer's Championship four times, not to mention innumerable stake matches, exhibitions, and minor tournaments. He holds the world's scoring record for thirty-six holes—132, made at Wolf Hollow.

In 1929 he won the British Open but lost in the U. S. Open and the P. G. A. He has never had a season as brilliant as Bobby Jones had winning the British Amateur and Open and the U.. S. Open successively, but there seems to be some foundation for the belief that at match play Hagen is still better than Atlanta's golfing lawyer. When the pair met in the South and played one round over Jones's course at Sarasota and another over Hagen's course at Pasadena, it was a dull match. Hagen, the gambler, the opportunist who in most of his matches never stops trying to turn threes into twos, played as if no one else were on the course. He tried for par and got it, while Jones, knowing Hagen's penchant for taking chances, decided to take the chances himself, discarded his faultless conservatism for gambler's golf, and took fives and sixes. When twelve holes of the match were left to play Jones was twelve down. They played onto the thirteenth green. Jones had a six-foot putt for a four. Hagen had a twenty-five-foot putt. There was no need for him to sink it. The match was practically his; if Jones won this hole, the big gallery would at least be able to watch them play one hole more. With his putter in the crook of his elbow, studying his little putt, Jones saw Hagen's ball wind its long course square into the hole. . . .

In the crowd that walked back to the clubhouse that afternoon was a gentleman famous in another branch of sport, Mr. John McGraw. "What do I think of Walter Hagen?" he said to the press man who strolled beside him. "I'll tell you what I think of him. I think he's a great baseball player gone to waste. . . ."

Mr. McGraw's remark was not meant as a reflection on the champion's golf. He had detected in his lounging frame, in his eyes which, at once speculative, restless, and self-absorbed, seem to be watching something that will happen in a minute, in his walk, in his easy stances, in the slight, unorthodox roll of his swing, timed to give the fullest possible leverage to the loose muscles sliding under his silk shirt, that balance of relaxation and energy which is the quality of the born athlete. And Mr. McGraw's remark is given additional patness by the fact that for a long time golf, to Walter Hagen, was only a back road to the baseball diamond.

The back road started on Myrtle Avenue in Rochester, New York, and ran down a hill and along the wire fence, bordered with shrubbery, that defined the boundaries of the Rochester Golf and Country Club. The high-school baseball team for which Walter Hagen pitched had its field near the golf course and, on his way to practise on spring afternoons, he looked over the fence and saw the club members swinging at little balls with long thin sticks. Behind these swingers walked boys he knew, caddying. Some of them earned two dollars a day. Walter Hagen was a good pitcher—one of the best the Rochester team ever had—and he had no idea of deserting baseball when he, too, began to spend some of his time as a caddy. In the beginning he only wanted money enough to buy a new baseball uniform, but pretty soon he began to play the game and found that it offered possibilities. He became assistant to the professional at the Rochester Club and then took a job as professional in the Oakland Hills Club in Detroit. His game had become very good. In 1913 he entered the National Open.

He finished fourth. That was the year that Harry Vardon and Ted Ray, the Englishmen, tied with Francis Ouimet for the championship and were beaten by Ouimet in a play-off that made the latter young man a national hero. In the shuffle nobody paid any attention to Hagen. He was hailed as a man from nowhere when, the next year, he won the Open at Chicago.

He was to have one more contact with baseball before it passed permanently out of his career. The following spring, practising golf in Jacksonville, he met a man he knew who had come South to join the training camp of the Philadelphia National League baseball team. This friend suggested that Walter Hagen come out and do some pitching, and for several weeks he played baseball with the Phillies. He did so well that before the team went North he was offered a contract. He turned it down. There was, he decided, more money in golf.

Events have borne out his decision. His yearly income is a good deal more than Babe Ruth's. He makes over $10,000 a year in prize money (an average of the last few years), $45,000 from his exhibition matches, and his salary as golf expert of the Pasadena Golf and Country Club was $35,000. Add it up.

His ambition was expanding with his reputation, and in 1919, as American Open Champion, accompanied by a valet, three trunks full of clothes, and a resonant ballyhoo, he went to England and played in the Open at Troon. He finished fifty-fifth. Various reasons were advanced to account for his poor showing; as sensible as any is the theory that the prestige, the supposed insuperability of the British players, keyed him up to taking too many chances. But every day, no matter how bad his score was, he posted his card.

Even when he is playing badly Hagen's mag-
netism keeps the gallery watching him. Al Watrous
tells a story of how, in a tournament at the Olympia
Fields Club in Chicago, he saw John Farrell go by
on an adjacent fairway, followed only by his caddy.

"How y' doing, Johnny?" called Watrous.

"Wonderful," replied Farrell, who had been playing the best golf of his life and was leading the
tournament by a big margin. "I'm breaking the
course record."

"Where's your gallery?"

Farrell grinned.

"Over behind the clubhouse, watching Hagen play
mumblety-peg."

Hagen has never been popular in Great Britain.
In the first place he has never failed to show his in-
comprehension of the custom which forbids professional golfers (whose social status in England is not
much above that of a taxi starter) from entering
the clubhouse. Further, he has antagonized British
journalists by answering as frankly as he was able
the questions they put to him: his statements that
the famous course at Deal was not much more imposing than an ordinary seventy-two-par course and
that Englishmen were prone to dabble at golf did
not help his insular popularity. A story was even circulated to the effect that he had put his arm around

the championship cup where it stood on its graven pedestal and, addressing it as "baby," admonished it to "come to papa" because he was going to take it home with him. . . . In 1922 he replied as effectively as he could to his critics by winning the British Open at Sandwich.

A northwest wind was raking the course that day. Fine, salty rain veered in the gusts, flicking the golfers' faces and stiffening their hands. When Hagen went out to play the afternoon round he knew that he would have to take a thirty-six to win. Par was thirty-eight. He was continually off the course and continually making recoveries. On the sixteenth, a long, four-shot hole, his cause seemed hopeless. His second shot left him in the rough; he had a two-hundred-yard brassie shot to the green. He put his brassie shot next to the pin and sank his putt. "I think that shot," he says, "gave me the biggest kick I ever got out of golf."

It must be hard for him to decide what shot gave him the biggest kick; he has made a good many important ones. There was a shot in an exhibition match in which he had bet a thousand dollars that he would break the course record. The course record was sixty-nine. Hagen's sixty-seventh shot laid his ball on the eighteenth green, thirty feet from the cup. Hagen hit his putt and then, turning toward the men who had pooled their money against his, he permitted himself a piece of characteristic arrogance. "Do you think," he called, "I'd miss a putt like that for a thousand bucks? Not on your life. . . ." As he spoke he was strolling across the green. He did not even watch the ball on its slow roll. He knew that he had holed it.

He gave another instance of his bravado just before a match with Sarazen. They were going to play a course which Hagen had never seen but which Sarazen knew well. Hagen, who was suffering from a blistered foot, was afraid to make his foot worse by practising and equally afraid of letting Sarazen know that he was hurt.

"Come on out and I'll show you over the course," Sarazen suggested kindly the day before the match.

Hagen was sitting in the clubhouse with his bad foot on a chair.

"I'm sorry, Gene," he said, "I haven't time to look at your course. But I've sent my caddy out to look at it. . . ."

Even Sarazen's nerves were not proof against assurance like this. He lost his confidence and the match.

The jests of Walter Hagen are not always inspired by necessity. Once, having first made sure that no one was in the street, he dropped a golf ball out of

a window on the fourteenth floor of the Biltmore
Hotel to see how high it would bounce. It bounced
onto the roof of the Grand Central Station. . . .

Pranks like this delight him; he takes joy in any
happening which proves the world a place amenable
to wild deeds and legendary bounces, a place whose
obstacles one may challenge with one's wrist, bearing
reversals modestly and crowning triumphs with a
gasconade. Thus far the world has pretty well conformed to his pleasure. He has proved that, although
one may be married, an adult, and a voting citizen of
Pasadena, Florida, it is only necessary to play golf
three times a week to make $90,000 a year. He
could escape paying for anything he uses. Haber-
dashers, tailors, sporting-goods stores, and hotels
beg him to accept their best for nothing. The company that makes one small item of his apparel is
said to pay him a thousand dollars a year to wear it.
Whenever he arrives in a city it is apt to happen that
the agency of the most expensive automobile sold
in the locality calls up to offer him a car, and when
the car arrives he drives it himself at breakneck
speeds with great skill, roaring with laughter at the
tremors of his passengers. The principal article of
his luggage is an enormous golf bag, equipped with
ballwashers, special pockets for tees, gloves, sweaters, balls, medicines, and umbrellas, and containing

three solid silver putters, left-handed clubs for stymie shots, and a duplicate for every important club. It is the duty of his caddy, at the end of each day's play, to fit rubber covers over the grips of these clubs and then to place each club, grip and all, in a long flannel bag of the kind used to encase musical instruments.

In the title of this article I referred to Hagen as a Dutchman because he is of Dutch descent. The ancestors of his father (a landscape gardener in Rochester) spelled the name Haagen. It is true, of course, that neither the golfer's personality nor his behavior suits with the conventional notions of Dutch character; yet there is something about him that has always been characteristically Dutch, something reminiscent of the burgomasters who swaggered for Frans Hals, or Rembrandt's shadowy musketeers; something unqualified, indomitable. There is no better illustration of this quality than a moment in his play three years ago at St. Ann's.

Jones had won the tournament. At least, he had won it to all practical purposes. Hagen still had one shot left to play—a shot which, if he holed it, would give him a tie with Jones—and Hagen's ball lay in the fairway a hundred and fifty yards from the hole. The crowd, courteous to the loser, stood patiently enough, waiting for Hagen to play a shot that could have only one result, while his caddy, as if acting on instructions, left his side and walked up the lane of people toward the hole. Suddenly Hagen began to signal with his club. He wanted the caddy to take the flag out of the cup. . . .

A whisper ran through the gallery: "What's he want? What's he doing?" Most of the crowd saw quite well what he was doing. They questioned each other because they hardly dared believe what they saw. A hundred and fifty yards!

Down the narrow lane of green turf, with day closing round him and people pressed in rows on either side, Hagen, a little figure in this vista, was disclosing his intention of making a shot that no human being could expect to make. Very well—his gesture to the caddy seemed to say—if no human being could make this shot, then luck would make it for him, Walter Hagen, because he needed it. His mashie swung through its curve; the ball, perfectly lined, struck five yards from the hole, crawled a yard nearer, two yards, three yards, four yards . . . and stopped. And there the ball, having missed by a yard its impossible objective, lay still on the green turf like a small, round full stop, ending a legend.

FIRESIGN

FIRESIGN

FANNIE BRICE represents Broadway less by being its product than a comment upon it. Her talent, rare in that environment, is to make fakes look ridiculous, a talent she accounts for by saying that she had the luck to be born homely. That is not entirely true. At serious moments her face, with its green eyes and big mouth, is handsome, and she moves with a sort of awkward easiness that makes you wonder why the critics of her early efforts always called her homely. Perhaps they meant her nose. The operation that straightened and refined that organ a few years ago was the only mental or physical alteration in what nature made her that Fannie Brice has ever allowed.

It was an important operation. Besides the feminine instinct to make the best of herself, she had another, a professional reason, for wanting a nose less inevitably funny. She wanted to play serious parts, and accordingly, in 1926, New York saw a handsomer Fannie Brice dealing as well as she could with a play called *Fanny* which had its serious moments. Fairly successful in spite of its faults, it served principally to make people wonder what she could do if she ever got a good play. No matter what she does in serious work, however, she cannot keep people from thinking of her as a singer or from doubting whether she will ever find a theatrical vehicle that will equal in dramatic qualities the story of her own life.

Fannie Brice was born Fannie Borach in 1893, near Delancey Street. Her father, an Alsatian Jew, owned some saloons. Her mother, a Hungarian, helped run them, brought up the children, and cooked the free lunches. Fannie won five dollars singing "When You Know You're Not Forgotten by the Girl You Can't Forget" on amateur night in a Brooklyn theater. Later she sang in a stereopticon parlor in Eighty-third Street and then in a Cohan & Harris revue. Fired by Harris for bad dancing, she played one-night stands through Pennsylvania with a theatrical trainer named Rachel Lewis, trouped with a Hurtig & Seamon burlesque show, and was singing dialect songs by Irving Berlin as one of Spiegel's College Girls in the Columbia Burlesque house when Florenz Ziegfeld saw her and made her a head-liner in the *Follies*.

Fannie Brice was then seventeen. She had formally dedicated herself to the stage some time before when, tired of being called "More-Ache" and "Bore-Act" by her friends, she changed her name to Brice, the name of a friend of her mother's which

Fannie had liked when she heard it as a child. The reputation Ziegfeld was helping to procure for her under her new name opened the gateways for a career rich from the first in exciting circumstances. The streets in which she had grown up, the dark houses crowded with noises, accidents, and stubborn joys that civilization suppresses or ignores, had taught her a divided sympathy.

In those days she used to steal beer from her father to give to neighboring women who were sick or nursing; her outward, physical pity was supplemented by an altered but similar feeling directed toward herself. She wanted people to feel sorry for her. In a department store in which she worked for a while as a wrapper she told the girls her mother was dying and that her family was so poor they didn't have enough to eat. When the people in the store, believing her, offered bread and old clothes in sympathy, she came to work next day in her Sunday dress, wearing her mother's and sister's earrings, two earrings in each ear, and explained that she had only been fooling—her father was a millionaire.

Later, when she was on the road, truths suggested by the things she had done as a child became clear in her mind. "People like to feel miserable. You make them laugh they will forget you, but if you make them cry they will never forget you." As a burlesque trouper she was feeling, not altogether successfully, for a way to apply this belief to her work in the theater.

It still amuses her to remember incidents of her career. . . . One-night stands. . . . Feeding Rachel Lewis's dog on ten cents a day, eating herself on twenty-five. . . . Hotels: bribing the chambermaid before unpacking the electric stove, getting out of a window in Pittsburgh, stealing a curtain to use as a stage-wedding dress in Hazelton. . . . The night she caught Rachel jumping the show. . . . The night she joined the *Follies*. . . . Ten years of success, leading up to the night Ziegfeld came to her with a typewritten lyric in his hand and asked: "Do you think you can make them cry?"

Fannie Brice looked doubtful.

"I think you can," said the producer, handing her the song. "Just try it over once."

The accompanist rippled an introductory chord, and after a minute of study the girl sang the first lines of a lyric written by Channing Pollock for the French tune, "Mon Homme":

> It cost me a lot, but there's one thing that I've got:
> It's my man . . .

She sang it without gestures, her strong contralto giving an unforgettable reality to the crude words of the verse, the haunting, repetitive tune.

Neither Fannie Brice's appearance nor her early career had given her much opportunity for sentimental love affairs. Her most vivid memory of her first husband, a Springfield barber named White, was his liberal use of his own hair tonics. "God, he smelled nice!" She was not upset when her mother had the marriage annulled, shortly after it had taken place, on the ground that she was under age. She felt differently about Nicky Arnstein, whom she married in 1918. When he was accused of fraud and forgery, she did not believe the charges and gave little satisfaction to the district attorney who, cross-examining her in the Federal Building, tried to find out where he was hiding.

"Are you sure your memory is as bad as that, Miss Brice?"

"Yes, it is very bad. I can only remember songs and telephone numbers."

It was not calculated melodrama but pure accident that Arnstein came back to give himself up on the day when the police force of the city, which had spent weeks searching for him, paraded on Fifth Avenue. At nine that morning Fannie Brice met her husband by appointment at Ninetieth Street and Columbus Avenue and drove downtown with him. Several times they waited at corners, making jokes, while parts of the parade went by. "Recognize any friends, Nick?" . . . It was a warm, clear day, full of blue airs and snatches of band music; the two in the back seat seemed unconscious that it might be the last day they would spend together for some time. Five years later, when Arnstein got out of prison, they were reunited. In September, 1927, her faith broken at last, Fannie Brice abruptly divorced him in Chicago. The grounds were infidelity.

She has never expressed regret concerning her marriage or its epilogues, nor has she ever let what happened to her personally interfere with her work. Through good and bad times she continued to suggest her own songs, working out her ideas with someone who could build tunes around them. Some of the numbers which evolved from this system, with the collaboration of song writers like Willie Weston or Blanche Merrill, were "In the Spring," "Second-Hand Rose," "I'm an Indian," and the monologue, "Mrs. Cohen on the Beach." It is the peculiar quality of these numbers that they convince each hearer in the audience that he alone is capable of sensing the realism behind their lightness. At any rate, Fannie Brice thinks so and this is the effect she wants them to feel. Spontaneous when on the stage, varying her gestures and routine to suit her mood, she is keenly critical of her material, and when one of her songs is being discussed will analyze in detail its implica-

tions, thinking, like all good performers, from the
point of view of the audience.

Her impulse to comment on what she sees is not
limited in expression to singing songs or telling
funny stories. One day last winter she painted a picture in her dressing room. She worked in water
colors, later rubbing the paint with makeup to make
it look like oil. Fannie Brice exhibited it with
humorous comments to everyone who came in, but it
was not a silly picture. Her interest in line also applies to clothes. One of her principal amusements is
shopping. Three years ago, under the firm name
of Lottie & Brice, she was part owner of a dressmaking establishment in West Fifty-second Street.
She sold the place eventually because it took up too
much of her time, but it had been successful. She
has been known to say to a chorus girl, "Bring four
and a half yards of silk to rehearsal to-morrow, and
I'll make you a dress."

In such instances the dress, like her picture, was
made between changes of costume. At home she has
no time for these things because she is apt to be
busy with some detail of her apartment. Some curtains she had bought were not the right color. She
redyed them herself. She does not do these things
to save money but because they amuse her; she
spends her big salary almost as fast as she gets it,

giving a good deal of it away. Her generosity is noted even in a profession in which generosity is a tradition. All sorts of broken-down show people come to see her—girls who have been sick, song writers who can't write songs any more. One instance of her openhandedness concerns a racketeer who persuaded her to buy some diamonds. A crooked pawnbroker who had an agreement with the salesman had appraised the stones at double the price asked, but later they were identified by a more honest appraiser as paste. Two years afterwards Fannie Brice said with some excitement to a friend:

"You remember the guy that sold me those diamonds? He came round this afternoon."

Her friend remembered. "The dirty crook. Did you have him pinched?"

"No. I was foolish, I guess, but he was broke, he'd been in jail. I gave him a ticket back to Chicago."

Fannie Brice pays for her whims by a unique system of adjusting her own salary. Instead of arguments, her interviews with producers usually consist of a series of jokes on her part, of resistance and finally laughter on theirs, until somehow or other she has kidded them into giving her what she wants. Recently she made ten thousand dollars a week in a picture house, and her yearly earnings are around one hundred and fifty thousand dollars. She owns a Minerva, but lives modestly and quietly in an apartment hotel in East Sixty-ninth Street. Her only servant is a big colored maid named Gertie. For a while she sent her children, William Jules Arnstein and Fannie Arnstein, to private school, but now she sends them to public school because she thinks that is better for them. She has a place in Huntington, Long Island, but does not like it because the crickets keep her awake. She takes no formal vacations.

A few months ago she married Billy Rose, the song writer. Their mornings begin at one in the afternoon. She does not like to leave the house till her children are back from school; often her mother, who lives on the West Side and wears a picture of her daughter and her grandchildren embossed on a cameo brooch, comes over to eat and sometimes to cook the Brice luncheon. She is a famous cook, and Fannie Brice kids her about it. "Tell us what kind of soup you had last night, Ma. Was it golden?" While Rose waits to start downtown, she anxiously arranges the last details of her costume; she reads her mail in the car, at the same time making plans for the day, humming a tune she is learning, and looking out of the window. As the limousine moves toward Fifty-ninth Street, she keeps interrupting herself to call attention to people in the street, perpetually distracted and absorbed by the city of which her name, burning in golden letters through metropolitan evenings, is a characteristic, and in a way a permanent, part.

SKYBINDER

SKYBINDER

SEEING the Chanin brothers' name usually meant getting something in your eye, a piece of sand or ground rock from the construction job beside which the sign was nailed. The same name, with milder associations, confronted you in newspaper items describing real-estate deals. What the name stood for was not clear. Even when the old Manhattan Storage Warehouse was knocked down and the yellow pillar of a new building pushed up in terraces to a flagpole fifty-six stories above Murray Hill a good many people didn't know whether the Chanins were builders or, since the name was well known on Broadway, theater owners who had taken up building as a sideline.

Only about two years ago their reputation became familiar to those not immediately concerned with building or real estate. At that time a story was going round about a first-mortgage bond issue of six and a half million dollars which a bond house had put out to finance their new building. Because of the size of the sum, and because it was hard, just then, to sell any kind of bonds, preparations were made for a long, elaborate selling campaign; then the books were opened, and forty-eight hours later the whole issue had been subscribed. It was a dramatic indication that the public had heard of the Chanins.

The incident is impressive, for one thing, because builders are so rarely recognized. You can think of many architects and decorators who are well known, but the men who conceive the necessity for a building, who later carry out their conception, stay anonymous; the sign is torn off the employment shanty, and the finished skyscraper, its changing shadow in the air, itself takes on a personality as though it were some product of nature, obliterating those who made it. What is unusual about the Chanins' story is that their achievements are visible; a whole city of scattered buildings, a hundred and forty-one of them in New York and Brooklyn, including the Fur Center Building, Thirtieth Street Building, the Hotel Lincoln, the Mansfield, Majestic, Masque, Forty-sixth Street, Biltmore, Royale and Roxy Theaters, and the Chanin Building at Lexington Avenue and Forty-second Street. Many of these are still owned and managed by the Chanin Construction Company, an organization that includes four Chanin brothers: Irwin S. (thirty-eight), Henry I. (thirty-five), as equal, controlling partners; Sam (thirty-two), and Aaron (twenty-eight) in minor capacities. Henry, a trained accountant, attends to the business organization; Irwin, the engineer, plans the actual construction. Irwin is the one who makes the plans; he started things in the first place, and the story of the Chanins' rise is really his story.

Trying to find a detail that will tell something about Irwin Chanin, I can only say what has been said of many business men: that he has most of the characteristics of a competent artist. That this has been said so often suggests a rule: there is a certain kind of intelligence which, though concerned with making money, is essentially an artist's intelligence, and the work of industrialists who have this kind of brains is often so concentrated that it resembles the work of creative art. But though Irwin Chanin may work and think like an artist, he does not look like one.

He is a small, dark-skinned man whose bald forehead and tight clothes make his face look big in proportion to his body. He wears glasses, the two halves of which are connected by an arching gold bar; you notice this because his eyes, prominent and intense, underlined with slight shadows, are the most striking feature of his face. When talking about something that interests him he jumps out of his chair and walks around a room, illustrating his ideas with gestures and pantomime; at such times his speech is full of metaphors borrowed from the building profession. He has a small mustache and wears a ring with a big colored stone. Henry is quieter, better-looking; Sam, and Aaron, who was hurt in the Times Square subway accident two years ago, are normal, healthy young Jews. Although they are seen together as a rule only on important family occasions, all four brothers were photographed on the roof of the Chanin Building the day Irwin drove the ceremonial golden rivet that completed the steel frame. I got an idea then what they must have looked like twenty-four years ago, arriving with their parents in Ellis Island from Poltava, Russia.

It was the second Chanin immigration. The first had taken place some twenty years before that, when Simon Chanin, the father, came to try his luck in Bensonhurst, a suburb of Brooklyn. He had made money as a contractor and after saving ten thousand dollars had gone back to Poltava, a sensible move, since with his capital he could live there like a rich man. Because the kids had been born in America the government school wouldn't take them; they went to a private school where Irwin, praised by his teachers, decided he would be an engineer. Simon Chanin favored the idea. He saw that going home had not been so smart after all. Faraway warnings of the revolution, beginning to be felt in Russia, had made even the best investments shaky; he had lost most of his ten thousand dollars. So in 1907 the Chanins came back to Bensonhurst, where Henry went to a business school and Irwin to Cooper Institute. The war interrupted the jobs they were holding after graduation. In 1919 Henry, who had been wounded directing a machine-gun battery, got a bookkeeping job in Washington; Irwin, who had been in base camps here, went home. As many other young men were doing then, he lived in his father's house and tried to figure out some way to make a living.

During that winter he took stock of what he could do. He had, he remembered, won three scholarships in Cooper Institute and a special prize for designing a double-track railroad bridge. He had worked for his father on building jobs and later for a subway contractor. More recently, on the government job, he had helped to build a factory for poison-gas near Cleveland, Ohio; here he had been educated to the importance of speed. The major under whom he had worked sent him a telegram offering him a civilian job at a hundred a week. Chanin refused because he thought that somehow he would find a way to make more money himself.

In spite of the general depression of business at that time, the builders around Bensonhurst were making money buying land and putting up cheap houses on it. The method was to finish the houses outside and let the buyer decide how he wanted them inside. The houses were almost all alike, thin-walled, with new sidewalks, lawns without grass, imitation hardwood paneling. Chanin went with the salesmen who were showing the houses and listened to the criticisms of the customers. He thought of improvements that would make houses of this kind look better and decided that if he could raise the money he would go into the building business himself.

Now came the first step in his rise, a step which at the time it was carried out seemed, and was, an almost impossible feat. Somehow Chanin raised the money to build two houses at ten thousand dollars apiece. The man who owned the lots had been asking a thousand dollars down payment; he let them go for a hundred. A hundred dollars was all the money Chanin had. He borrowed the life-savings of the girl he was engaged to—about three hundred dollars. Friends of his father lent him enough to bring his capital up to a thousand. He borrowed the remaining nineteen thousand from local bankers by showing them the major's telegram and convincing them that if his scheme was a failure he would pay them back in other ways. He started to build the houses. Most of the carpenters and plasterers working for him had cars; he had none and so he rode out to the job every day on a bicycle. He was successful. The artistic details of construction which he had planned with such joy had the effect he had estimated; he sold the houses before they were finished for a six-thousand-dollar profit; a little later he wrote to Washington and asked his brother Henry to come home to look after the office work of his expanding projects.

In the next year the brothers put up twenty houses in Bensonhurst and a forty-tenant apartment house that was immediately rented to capacity. Other builders copied their cottages and went on copying them after the demand had been filled. The Chanins figured these builders would sell out for a loss. A tenant would buy for ten thousand dollars a two-family house that in normal times would cost thirteen or fourteen thousand; he would rent half of it for enough to pay all his expenses. He would tell his friends about his good luck until, by degrees, a new market would be created for the little houses. This was exactly what happened. The Chanins had traded their apartment house, heavily mortgaged, for rows of two-family houses left unfinished by a discouraged builder. They sold these houses, built garages, stores, markets to go with them, and then decided there was nothing more for them to do in Bensonhurst.

By this time they had an office in Brooklyn. It was small and dark, the rent was high. The Chanins went to a title company to get financing for an office building. An old friend, one of the title company's vice presidents, tried to persuade them to give up their foolhardy scheme. Brooklyn didn't need any more office buildings, and if it did, why should they build them? Irwin Chanin called the vice president's stenographer and dictated a prediction of the profits to be made in office buildings. He said he would come back in a year and have it read, but even eight months later this became unnecessary. By that time the Chanins had started and already sold two buildings and were beginning to study values in New York.

The Fur Center Building was their first project on this side of the river. They had found that the wholesale fur trade, concentrated in the West Twenties, needed new quarters. Their building, supplying an old demand, made money right away, and Irwin Chanin turned his attention to theaters.

For the past few years he had been using his imagination principally to detect business opportunities. He saw that at that time, unlike the present, there was a need for more theaters. This alone would have been enough to make him build theaters of his own, but he had another inducement as well.

His interest in plays, as in most forms of artistic expression, had set him thinking about theaters a long time before. As a boy he had sat in the gallery, going in by a side door. He had always disliked that. In his own theaters everyone would go in by the same door. Building them, he revived the talent for unusual detail that had made him successful in the early days in Bensonhurst; he made the orchestra and balcony seats unusually wide and comfortable. He saved space in the entrance foyers, improved the acoustics and gave the actors better dressing rooms. He got so interested that he hired David Burton as play director and began backing plays himself. Sometimes he put up all the money; sometimes another producer shared the risk. Before he quit, Chanin lost an amount variously estimated at between twenty-five and thirty thousand dollars.

Puppets of Passion, a brilliant success in Europe, was his worst flop as a producer. He made up for it immediately with a new idea, bigger than any of his others. Late one night, instead of going home to Brooklyn, the brothers called up six New York hotels to get a room and found they were all full. Here, obviously, was the suggestion for a new investment, and the Chanins put up the thirty-story Hotel Lincoln at Eighth Avenue and Forty-fourth Street.

For some time now, S. W. Straus & Company had

been backing almost all the Chanins' ventures in New York. With money in the bank and new confidence in his own ideas, Irwin gave up all pretense of routine and worked night and day on plans, details. He drew pictures himself of the kind of furniture he wanted in the lobby of the Lincoln, sofas and chairs the curves and angles of which represented the roofs and bridges of the city. He designed one frieze to show the shadow of a line of skyscrapers falling across a street, and another the motif of which is the tire of a Mack truck. He had lamps made to look like safes and a fountain like an office building. He wasn't satisfied with making designs; he sometimes worked even on the material of the decorations, taking the brush out of a painter's hand to show him what he wanted.

Naturally, he isn't precise—no artist-industrialist understands efficiency in its customary sense. Irwin Chanin's activities confuse his employees; his secretary, for instance, cannot make any guess at the time he will give each appointment. With a list of people waiting to see him he may go out with the first one who comes and work with him till midnight. But his organization, too, is one of the things the details of which absorb him; once a year he calls in each of his employees to hear complaints or suggestions.

He has made up a set of aphorisms which he frequently quotes. "If you give people the best you can, and don't worry, they will get anxious and come running after you and give you money and everything." "Money is the easiest thing in the world to get. You just have to have ideas and it will come to you—why, it will pour in." Coming from a man well known for his ability to drive a bargain, these statements are, nevertheless, probably sincere. I don't believe he does think first about money, but about ideas for getting money, and his enthusiasm is for the success of the idea to which money is a testimonial.

With real-estate holdings worth close to one hundred million dollars, Henry and Irwin Chanin lived for years in a big unpretentious apartment in an apartment house they own on Ocean Avenue, Brooklyn; their father and mother live in Bensonhurst. In the mornings, Irwin drives to business in his Pierce or his Cadillac or, if he is late, gets into the subway at Atlantic Avenue. He smokes cigarettes, rarely drinks. Married in 1920 to a girl from Bensonhurst, he has three children and a country place in Davenport, Westchester; he plays golf once in a while but likes fishing and swimming better. Every Saturday and Sunday in the summer he goes fishing in Peconic Bay; the rest of the time he works, as usual, eighteen hours a day. He and Henry sign checks on a joint business account. Each is insured for a million dollars for the benefit of the Chanin Construction Company.

I have left out a lot of facts about Irwin Chanin that are interesting but that fit too neatly into the success stencil. His career is not important because it is so typical of successful careers, but because it is a good portrait of the type of big-businessman who has the talents and impulses of an artist. A story that illustrates best what I mean is one he tells to illustrate something else: how, when the Chanin Building was almost finished, he took two friends, a painter and sculptor, to the roof. He showed them first all the details he prizes so much: the twenty elevator cabs, all different, all made of imported woods usually used only for jewel boxes and violins; the theater for industrial conferences on the fiftieth floor. When at last they climbed an iron ladder onto the topmost terrace he said nothing, but stood watching their faces while they looked at the view.

"Why, they looked around—you know what you can see? They looked around, like that—they were struck dumb. . . ."

Imitating their expressions, he opens his mouth and eyes wide, lifts his hand. But somehow he manages to suggest not his friends' but rather his own perpetual wonder and excitement at what he has done, the excitement of an artist at an achievement which, its many details forgotten in the whole, seems like a miracle.

Now he has plans made for the biggest building in the world, a hotel with six thousand rooms which will rise somewhere near the middle of town. He won't talk about it until the foundation is laid, a partly superstitious reticence which resembles that of composers and writers who won't talk about what they are working on. Buildings to him are ideas, at once more concrete and more abstract than they are to other people. At first it is hard to see why this is so or to realize the logic of the connection between this active, unsystematic, bald, and high-strung little man and the big, quiet buildings he has made, but after thinking about it for a minute you understand it.

JAZZ JELLY

JAZZ JELLY

PAUL WHITEMAN and Fritz Kreisler, arm in arm on a Berlin street corner. . . . Paul Whiteman in the Kit-Kat Club. . . . Paul Whiteman and Max Reinhardt. . . . Paul Whiteman and Rachmaninoff. . . . Such pictures as these, appearing in the press with increasing frequency throughout the last four years, have sufficiently attested to the fact that Paul Whiteman has a good publicity man. And when, one winter evening, Paul Whiteman brought jazz to Carnegie Hall and celebrated there its ultimate mysteries before an audience notable for the absence of tin-pan alley, it was clear that his fame had borne its fruit. Previous to that evening he had been an amusing mountebank. Now the newspapers took him seriously. People began to wonder whether Paul Whiteman might not be taking himself seriously, too.

That was hard to believe. It seemed unkind to suspect that such a bladderish man could regard his antics as culturally significant. He is fat. Great musicians are not fat. Music, which consumes the hearts, wastes also the flesh of its adorers. And Paul Whiteman, with his look of a Dutch miller—

no, you couldn't see him as stylist. But one thing
was clear—Paul Whiteman had made himself, in
name at least, the foremost exponent of an immensely important development in music. To what
did he owe that position?

The question was asked by a reporter who went
to see him after the concert. He wanted, he said, to
write a success story about Mr. Whiteman. Could
Mr. Whiteman give him something that he could
work into an anecdote? Merrily, with his small eyes
snapping above his great pale cheeks, Paul Whiteman told about the place where he had first heard
jazz. It was in Africa, at Capper's Neptune Palace.

He had come a long way to Capper's gay doorway,
vibrant with drums in the tropical night. There had
been Denver, where his father was director of
musical education in the public schools and where
he, Paul, had learned to play the viola; then San
Francisco where, in a year of gun salutes, prize
cattle, and confetti, the aged Saint-Saëns conducted
a new symphony with the World's Fair Orchestra.
Paul Whiteman played in that orchestra. When the
Fair ended he joined an organization composed of a
French 'cello who had failed in the restaurant business, a yellow Hungarian fiddle, and a bass viol with
carbuncles who remembered Garibaldi. They toured.
Finally their wanderings led them to Africa and a

town called Cobra. And in Cobra, Paul Whiteman
heard strange noises issuing from Capper's dance
hall, and followed them inside.

The quartet broke up in Cobra and for a while
Paul Whiteman worked in Capper's. Going north
again he found that jazz had come to San Francisco.
He worked for a while in Tait's restaurant, was
fired for "not knowing how to jazz," started a band
of his own, and after many difficulties, borrowed
money and brought his men east to play in the Am-
bassador Hotel in Atlantic City. When the Victor
Phonograph Company held a convention in that
resort one of the vice presidents, impressed with
Whiteman's playing, invited him to make some
records. Three months later he was famous.

He had not done anything very startling to the
music he was playing, except that he insisted on
rehearsing it like a symphony piece with thoughtful
instrumentation. His pianist, Ferdie Grofé, a brilliant technical musician, who had joined the
orchestra in San Francisco, made his arrangements;
Whiteman's contributions to the general effect were
always thought up at rehearsals. He can tell very
little about a composition from reading it, but when,
with his shirt unbuttoned and the visor of a golf
cap pushed round to the back of his neck, he hears his
men play something for the first time, his mind

begins to work, and he gives the score its finishing touches—here a comedy trumpet, there a banjo swipe. The first record he made for the Victor Company—"Avalon" and "Dance of the Hours"—was spoiled in repeated trials by the audible soft oaths of players cursing their own mistakes. None of them swore at the result, for records made the Whiteman Orchestra very popular. Even people who didn't go to the Palais Royal heard of Paul Whiteman; he began to get invitations to play at private parties. One evening he found his men clustered in the vestibule of a big house while a liveried servant, obscure and speculative, watched them through the curtain of the glass front door.

"He wants us to go round to the service entrance, Paul," a trombone player explained, jerking his thumb at the embattled lackey. Whiteman sought out the host. His players, he said, were gentlemen. They would go round to nobody's back door. On another night, in the house of a celebrated soup manufacturer, he refused, with equal firmness, to have his men fed in the pantry. They weren't waiters, they were artists, equals of the best, blowing beauty, making good pay.

Every important musician who has heard his orchestra has been amazed by the individual brilliance of the players. "Who does this?" demanded

Rachmaninoff. "Who has taught them?—An orchestra of virtuosos." The secret of such playing is not as recondite as a Russian mind might fancy. Paul Whiteman has the best players because he pays them more than anyone else can afford to. He paid his former saxophone, Russ Gorman, between forty and fifty thousand a year.

When Leon Goossons, the best clarinet in Europe, came to the New York Symphony, Whiteman remarked, "If he's any good I'll get him away from the Symphony and give him a taste of real jack!" He has performed this simple favor for innumerable symphony men; Chester Hazlett, saxophone, was clarinet in the San Francisco Orchestra; Walter Bell, his contra-bassoon, has written three symphonies; Frank Sigrist, a trumpeter with a four-inch lip, also played with him on the West Coast. With symphony orchestras they were making sixty dollars a week, with Whiteman they make two hundred and fifty dollars and up. Such men are aristocrats, the flower of their profession.

Paul Whiteman has told in his book, *Jazz*, how at supper time at a party of Lord Mountbatten's he caught a drummer hurrying out of the room.

"Let go of me," said the percussion artist, edging away from Whiteman's anxious grasp. "I'm going out to wire my old man that the Prince of Wales has served me champagne with his own hands."

This spacious evening has been supplemented by others—the night in Berlin when two rows of students, holding tankards of pilsener, formed outside the stage door and made him drink right and left as he passed between them; the night in Vienna, when he sat in the Royal Box and heard the bandmaster of the late Emperor Franz Joseph conduct a special program of Viennese waltzes; the night in Kansas City when a girl threatened to commit suicide unless he gave her an introduction to David Belasco. Brass bands in airplanes swooped over the steamer that brought him up the harbor one August. In his apartment, and in his office over Broadway, he plunged back into rapid rhythms. He goes to bed at three. He gets up at nine.

In the mornings he does business, looks after the affairs of his half dozen orchestras; in the afternoons he rehearses or works on scores; in the evenings he records at the Victor laboratory or plays at a party. His personal income, about three hundred thousand dollars a year, is perhaps the world's best illustration of the truism to the effect that those who dance must pay the piper.

Everyone borrows from him; he is owed more money than any other man in music.

Besides the money he pours out to those who ask his charity, he spends big sums for motor cars, for apartments he never lives in, for clothes he never wears, and, above all, for parties. Every Christmas he gives a notable reception which never costs less than three thousand dollars and never breaks up until breakfast is on the table. He has one child, Paul Whiteman, Jr.

And here, at thirty-nine, is Paul Whiteman, a man flabby, virile, quick, coarse, untidy, and sleek, with a hard core of shrewdness in an envelope of sentimentalism, striped ties, perspiration, and fine musical instincts. He smokes incessant Chesterfields. He weeps at the opera. He does not, himself, dance.

His life has been a succession of other people's parties. But sometimes, when a piano is clicking in his apartment, he shouts at his third wife (she was Vanda Hoff, the dancer): "Come on, Mother, do the Charleston." At such times, in the warmth of his joviality, he seems inert, inconsequential; when he conducts, a recognizable concentration asserts itself and he seems to have two faces—a tight, inner face pushing out through the mild nimbus of a front too big for it. The anxiety that sharpened him in the early days, making him alert to a musical development clouded under the vapidity of the early ragtime has gone; it has been replaced in him by the acceptance of a musical responsibility. Perhaps, now, he would not be so sensitive to the whisper of a new and formless music, elusive and unknown. He is more concerned with the handling of what lies concretely under his baton. He has achieved his goal—money; to reach it he became an artist. There is no disputing the fact that modern dance music owes to him much of its sophistication; he is directly responsible for the artistic recognition of jazz and for many of its instrumental methods; his influence is obvious in numberless orchestras. Whiteman was, however, rather the agent than the initiator of the force that raised him.

He is still doing it. He does it with a twitching elbow and a little stick—a pudgy palm flattening the strings, an eyebrow crooking up the brasses. He has said that nobody can lead a jazz band with a baton—it must be done with the head, and when he begins to play his head nods to rhythm like the head of a mechanical mandarin. As the music rises his whole body shakes and wabbles; his waistcoat buttons strain at their fastenings; warm discords pass in shimmers through his flesh. "Jazz Jelly," Olin Downes called him, and the phrase was taken up with enthusiasm by the critics who watched his antics on the night of his triumph, as he led the climactic ending of the "Rhapsody in Blue" upon the dais of Carnegie. The critics, at that moment, were solemn. They were thinking up adjectives. Neither to them nor to Paul Whiteman, intent upon his score, did anything matter that had preceded that moment; what parties had passed by, with drums rustling, fiddles sighing their faint and gay nostalgia out of lighted windows, what yellow nights, what numberless tunes had gone past, worn out by dancing feet, to leave him there, a vehement, thick figure, whipping sound to a point. His baton stopped. A storm fluttered the pale hands behind him. Turning, he bowed.

RED HOT

RED HOT

HARRY STEVENS belongs to the class of men who have grown rich by creating a national necessity. Like the inventors who brought quick transportation and electric light into the lives of everyone, he has discovered something and popularized it. He has given this country the hot dog.

In square block capitals the top of his letterhead is this:

HARRY STEVENS
PUBLISHER : CATERER

a seemingly simple statement which needs an explanation. To understand thoroughly what it means you would have to go around with Harry Stevens for fourteen hours of any summer day. This is his busy season, for in the summer people gather in big crowds out of doors, and crowds have to be fed. With the ball parks open for baseball in the afternoons and once in a while for a prizefight in the evenings, with special trains going out every day to some track near the city where the horses are running, Harry Stevens hurries from one place to another. He has the catering concessions at many ball parks and almost a dozen tracks. As for what he publishes, well, he publishes score cards and programs. From the sale of one thing and another, mostly hot dogs, he has made several million dollars.

It would be easy to write an essay showing how Harry Stevens belongs in a way that is freakish, but not funny, to a class of men from whom Woolworth and Ford have sprung, men who have started something growing and grown big fortunes with it and who, more daring but less hopeful than the backwoods pioneers, eliminate—like all pioneers— the conditions that would produce their own type in the future. But an essay would be a dull way to do it; to describe Harry Stevens is to describe in most of its details the type to which he belongs, against its usual background of early poverty, of luck helped by shrewdness, of hardness, energy, sensitiveness, simplicity, distrust, and humor.

Harry Stevens is sixty-nine years old. He usually wears a blue suit of some heavy, expensive material which looks dusty because of the cigar ashes he keeps dropping over it. His head is covered with strong gray hair which he parts on the side; one lock in the shape of a triangle drops over his right eyebrow. When he talks he gesticulates and is apt to quote Shakespeare. He is square-shouldered and as a young man he was very strong; he still has great endurance and can stand on his feet all day, looking after business in one of his offices or kitchens. He has the sole right to sell hot dogs, sandwiches, and pop at the Yankee Stadium, the Polo Grounds, Ebbets Field, both ball parks in Boston, Swayne Field in Toledo, the Coliseum in Chicago, the International Polo matches, Empire City, Saratoga, Belmont, and four tracks in Maryland, the six-day bicycle races, the Automobile Show, and twenty or thirty other arenas.

The fact that from one thing and another he has made several million dollars does not constitute his real success. His ability to estimate people and deal cordially with them has always been a more important part of his character than his ability to calculate. It has supported and partly created his business success and it has enriched his life more than anything else. In the course of his business he has met almost every sporting and political personage in the country and made most of them remember him and like him. Their photographs cover the walls of his Fifth Avenue office. He takes visitors round the gallery, stopping longest in front of pictures taken thirty years ago.

"That's Senator Hill, afterward the governor. A splendid gentleman, he was my friend. . . . There's my first staff at the Polo Grounds. See that big nigger out in front? Gorry, he was a son of a gun. . . . They're all dead now out of that picture except me."

There are photographs of Gene Tunney, Anton Lang, Lord Balfour, Father Murphy, Douglas Fairbanks, John McGraw, and many others, as well as cartoons by Bud Fisher and T. A. ("Tad") Dorgan. Harry Stevens's son Joe, who has his desk in the same room, would sometimes remind him of his social obligations.

"It's a long time since you called up Tad, Father."

"By God, it is," shouts Harry Stevens, and then to the telephone operator, "Get me Tad. . . . Hello, Tad, God bless you. . . . Great; how's yours? . . ."

He shouts on the telephone, but if anyone shouts at him he says crisply, "I'm not deaf." Every Christmas he used to send Tad Dorgan a box of cigars. He says the cartoonist did more than anyone else to make hot dogs popular.

"I just discovered them. Dorgan named them."

It was Dorgan who introduced the name "hot dog" into his cartoons, making it one of those wisecracks which issued from the mouths of his characters in the form of puffs of smoke. He was taking advantage of the popular belief that butchers put stray curs into their sausage machines, but though

the name caught on right away it did not for some
reason keep people from eating the commodity sold
by Harry Stevens. On the contrary, they bought
it faster. Sausages in rolls had been sold before
Stevens sold them. But never with mustard—never
in quantity—never to sporting crowds.

One cold day at the Polo Grounds, in 1900, Harry
Stevens sold his first hot dog. It was his son Frank's
idea that the crowds would want something hot. A
sandwich made of sliced meat couldn't be kept hot
but the skin cover on a sausage keeps the heat in.
Stevens began selling sausages in rolls, and even
with Dorgan making fun of them in cartoons, people
began asking for more.

But the sale of hot dogs, though important, was
only one factor in the success story that began one
day when Harry Stevens laid down fifty cents at
the ticket window of a ball park in Columbus, Ohio.

In the life of almost anyone a day or period can
be picked out which seems to have been a turning
point. That day in Columbus was a turning point
for Harry Stevens. He likes to remember his rise
from that time on and the years before that seem
meaningless as he looks back at them. He was born
in London, the son of a lawyer; he went to school
in Derbyshire. When he was twenty-one he married
and came to America. He had no money and no

trade. His wife had relatives in Niles, Michigan, and Stevens went there and got a job in an iron works. His wife bore him four sons and a daughter. He worked in the iron foundry until his union ordered a strike. Without a job, he didn't see at first what he could do.

A red-faced and thick-bodied young man in the high collar and round straw hat of the period, sitting with a score card in his hand under the hot Ohio sun in the wooden stand, he thought that the worst of his hard luck might be over. In his pocket was a book called *Irish Orators and Oratory,* which he had spent the morning peddling in the Firestone Buggy Works in Columbus. This was the best work he had found to do since the strike. For a while he had worked for a dollar and a quarter a day on the state road that ran through Niles; one evening he had seen an advertisement calling for salesmen for the book.

The ball game was slow that day, and Stevens shifted on the hard bench, stared at the people round him and at the program in his hands. He had been thinking about books, so he was critical of the card. It seemed to him an awkward kind of score card, hard to read; in the big ball parks they had advertisements on the score cards. . . . After the game he went to the manager of the ball park and asked if he could have the score-card concession. The manager said he could, for five hundred dollars. Stevens solicited advertising, got seven hundred dollars' worth of signed contracts. He gave five hundred dollars' worth of contracts to the manager instead of cash. He had discovered a business that would run without cash.

From that time on his story is a stencil. He moved from town to town, gambling without funds in score-card concessions and always succeeding. He went to Toledo, Cleveland, Milwaukee, Boston, Pittsburgh, and finally to New York. For a while he had the concession in Washington and got to know most of the congressmen who were baseball fans. Young Senator Hill always got a program from him at a certain place near the gate. Years later, when Hill was Governor of New York, there was a reception in his honor at the Polo Grounds. As the Governor passed through the stands to his box Stevens was standing on a bench selling programs.

"Hello, Harry," Hill shouted to him. "Have you changed your location?"

"No, sir," he said. "I just expanded."

He has kept on expanding. From his concession at the Yankee Stadium he moved out to the race tracks around the city. He began to contract for the catering privileges at the big fights. One by one he acquired the items of his imposing list of concessions.

Sometimes, when a race, a fight, and a ball game come on the same day, he caters to two hundred and fifty thousand people. His wieners are made to order by a wiener maker who sells to no one else. Stevens figures what he needs with great accuracy. After the Dempsey-Tunney fight in Philadelphia there were only sixteen ham sandwiches left in the baskets of his salesmen. When a lot of food is left he gives it to the Salvation Army.

He still comes down to work at nine every morning at his office at 320 Fifth Avenue. He has three sons in the business. The fourth son is president of a bank in Niles. His son Joe went to Yale and played on the ball team.

Harry Stevens was the last guest to leave the Savoy Hotel before it was torn down. He liked to sit with a cigar in a Fifth Avenue window watching the twilight rise out of the Park. He has a place in Niles facing the state road on which he used to work for a dollar and a quarter a day. His wife spends most of her time in Niles, and he takes his vacations there. He has never learned to play bridge or golf. He likes a game of pinochle. He has lived to see his organization spread halfway across the continent, with three printing presses working in each ball park to turn out his programs, with his custom-

made sausages keeping hot in patented nets and
inserted in rolls that have been split by a special
machine. He has lived to see his son Joe make a
two-base hit against Princeton with the bases full.
Dozing sometimes in his big chair, in his office
crowded with photographs, this heavy-handed,
rough-haired old gentleman, Harry Stevens, the man
who discovered the hot dog, looks back at life and
likes it.

BOSTONIAN THROUGH THE LOOKING-GLASS

BOSTONIAN THROUGH THE LOOKING-GLASS

S INCE it is something of a tradition in the theater for a producer to announce his permanent retirement every now and then, people who know Winthrop Ames were not particularly startled when he said that he was through with it all forever, that he was going to travel with his family and write a book. More interesting than the announcement itself was his own explanation of what had led him to make it. He said he thought he had done as good work in the theater as he ever would and that, believing this, he felt it pointless to continue in the business. Accordingly he sent back to their authors two plays he had planned to produce— Robert Sherwood's *Marching as to War* and a French play. He gave notice to all members of his force except an office boy, a telephone girl, and a stenographer. It was the melancholy gesture of a man who has spent his life straddling two worlds— Broadway and the world of money and leisure into which he was born; it was an acknowledgment that the world he had adopted was unsatisfactory after all, that it no longer paid him for the trouble he took with it.

Possibly the very fact that producing was not a business for Ames but an art, or a hobby, is a reason for not taking his retirement seriously. It isn't likely that he can find anything else that will give him as much fun. Producing plays did not provide him with a living, but it gave him something to work at happily, and at times even vigorously. How completely it absorbed him he showed only on rare occasions, such as a first performance of one of his plays, when he was too much concerned with the work in hand to maintain his habitual reserve. At such times, depressed and anxious, he hurried from place to place around the theater. He was usually obsessed with the idea that the piece wasn't moving fast enough; for an act he sometimes stood in the wings begging in a whisper for more speed. At the first performance of *Iolanthe* a friend found him behind a piece of scenery stimulating the chorus to dance faster by a command, inaudible on the stage, which he repeated wildly and monotonously: "Come on, you trollops." At other times he sat in the audience, muttering, swearing, and making corrections aloud, like some eccentric and dissatisfied spectator. Once a lady sitting behind him leaned forward and tapped him on the shoulder.

"We others in the theater want to listen to the play. If you don't like it, I advise you to go home."

Ames muttered an apology, took his hat, and went backstage, knowing it was beyond his power to sit quiet where he was.

His behavior was particularly bad at the first nights of his various revivals of Gilbert and Sullivan because of his great admiration for their works and because the old operas have an important meaning for him personally—associations drawn from the time when his mother took him to see *The Mikado*. He was sickly as a boy and had time to read a lot; his experience at the theater that night started an interest that went on through the years he spent at private school in Boston and later at Harvard, where he wrote the Hasty Pudding show and acted in it. At Harvard he met young men who stated boldly that when they got out they were going to be actors, and he discussed their chances of success with them; he knew he couldn't think of trying the stage himself. For three generations his family had been building up a business which had made them rich— the Ames Shovel & Tool Company. It was taken for granted that he would go into the tool works. He had given enough proof of his artistic tastes to be taken seriously when he insisted that he wasn't fit for business, but the greatest variation from tradition that the family permitted him was a routine job on a magazine, the *Architectural Review*.

He worked for the *Architectural Review* for six years. It was dull stuff. One day, after a good dinner, he went to a hotel lavatory to brush up and there confronted himself unexpectedly in the looking-glass. Resting one hand on a washbasin, he studied the face in front of him, silently asking himself questions. He believes that the ten or twelve seconds he spent standing there and staring at himself were decisive moments in his life. His reflection answered his silent questions, saying that he was bored and getting nowhere, and that the only thing he wanted to do was get into the theater business. He decided to tell the editor of the architectural magazine that he was leaving. A few days later he proposed to a friend of his that they pool as much money as they could raise and take over the old Castle Square Theater which was then up for sale. His acquaintance, another Boston society man who shared his taste for dramatics, fell in with the plan; they bought the theater and did business there with more or less success for several years.

By the time he left Boston for New York he had made a reputation as a producer. He ignored the pressure of those of his relatives who had been first amazed and then indignant that a descendant of Roger Winthrop and a nephew of a Governor of Massachusetts should enter a trade which was, in their opinion, undignified and vaguely dirty. He retained his inherited shares in the Ames Shovel & Tool Company and instituted the practice he still continues of drawing his considerable income without bothering to attend directors' meetings. He had come to New York at the request of the men who had just built the New Theater, the same imposing edifice at Central Park West and Sixty-second Street which has been known for the past decade as the Century. Most of the backers of the New Theater were boxholders of the Metropolitan Opera Company who had discovered that they stood to lose money on the venture. They were determined to go through with their plans, however, so as to keep faith with the people who had taken boxes, and got Ames in to take charge.

The project was the most expensive failure in the history of the American theater up to that time. Ames tried to let his new associates down as easily as possible, but couldn't do much to help them. Carrying out the original idea for the theater, he had to produce plays and light opera at high prices, although he recognized that only vaudeville or popular musical comedy—since this was before moving pictures had developed much—could have filled the twenty-five hundred seats of the big house. By the time his contract was up, he had developed an aversion for big theaters that has lasted all his life. His Little Theater in West Forty-fourth Street has only two hundred and ninety-nine seats. He built it with his own money after leaving the New Theater. Its success was undoubtedly one of the chief stimulants of the little-theater movements that were soon flourishing in other cities. He opened it with *The Pigeon* and went on to present John Barrymore in *The Philanderer*; as a sponsor of Schnitzler and Shaw and Galsworthy, none of whom was then familiar to his audience, he became the only producer in whose taste the literary type of critic and the literary type of playgoer had perfect confidence.

Undoubtedly Ames was able to set his artistic standards as high as he liked, because he was not in the theater business to make money; his inherited share in Ames Shovel & Tool made him a very rich man. On the other hand, as he frequently stated, he was not in the theater business to lose money. Producing would not have amused him if he had not imposed on himself the conditions imposed on other producers by necessity: if the public, after a two weeks' trial, didn't like a play of his, he took it off. His competence as a workman kept him from being a dilettante, just as his private fortune kept him from being a professional; the theater was neither his hobby nor, strictly, his business; I suppose it may be best defined as his occupation. Sometimes he produced a play that appealed to him artistically, although he knew it had no chance of commercial success—such a play as Philip Barry's *White Wings*. Sometimes, on the other hand, he put on something he didn't care for much himself but felt that he ought to produce because people would go to see it. He recognized *The Green Goddess* as skillful claptrap but staged it because it was a good vehicle for his friend George Arliss. He made more money out of it than out of any of his other productions. In twenty years of producing he has broken only a little better than even financially.

In his continuous search for new plays he perfected an elaborate reading system. Reports on more than ten thousand plays that had been read by his staff were filed in a special room next to his private office. A synopsis in two or three sentences was made of every play submitted to him; Ames read these synopses himself, and if he liked the idea read the manuscript even if his reader had indicated that it was not worth producing. He wrote letters to the authors of all rejected plays—tactful little notes that probably made numbers of inept playwrights believe that they had talent. Curiously enough, all his care did not bring efficient results; twenty per cent of the plays read by one member of his staff were afterward staged by other managers. *Street Scene* passed through his office without rousing enough interest to make its rejection remembered. After William A. Brady had produced it with a success that culminated in the Pulitzer Prize, Ames's casting director and chief reader, Johnson Briscoe, stated his surprise that Elmer Rice hadn't offered the play to Ames.

A secretary examined the manuscript record and reported that he had.

"Who turned it down?"

"You did."

The record showed that *Street Scene* had been rejected because its essential situation was not strong enough and because in general it was not the sort of thing Ames liked to do.

From Ames's point of view, the rejection was not a mistake; *Street Scene* was not his style. He never produced realistic dramas about poor people because he felt he didn't know the background; he never produced comedy because he didn't think he had the right touch. He can explain convincingly why this or that was beyond his ability, but in the last analysis his trick of endless self-depreciation comes down to a lack of self-confidence.

He is shy of talking in public. When called before the curtain on a first night, his gratitude for present favors and avowal of aims for the future, impeccably

expressed, could rarely be heard beyond the sixth
row; at rehearsal the ordeal of telling forty or fifty
people how to play their parts so oppressed him that
on the day of a first rehearsal he rarely ate, knowing that if he did he would get indigestion. His talent
for economy was practised vigorously in his professional life. He always arrived at the theater accompanied by a secretary who carried a huge bronze
ashtray, not for the sake of ostentation, but because
Ames rehearsed his companies in theaters which he
owned himself and, being frugal, shrank from pressing butts into the rugs. He liked to joke with money
in the manner of the elder Rockefeller; after a
good rehearsal of one of his Gilbert and Sullivan
productions he gave the whole company a two-cent
raise, and this amount was duly handed out in bright
pennies with each pay-check for the run of the
show.

When he wasn't putting on a new show his office
hours—starting at about eleven and lasting till six
or seven—were irregular, but the work he did was
regular and monotonous in the extreme. He went
over the synopses of the plays that had come in and
selected some to read himself. He read an average
of twenty plays a month. He had a little apartment
over his office in the annex of the Little Theater in
West Forty-fourth Street—a bedroom, dining room,

and kitchen. He kept a housekeeper there. A private stairway went down to the office on the floor below, an office that suggested the word "chambers"; the walls wainscoted in oak; beside his desk a big leather armchair and beside the chair a table with cigars and cigarettes on it. Everyone on his payroll at the time of his retirement had been with him for years, and when one of them had a birthday the event was celebrated upstairs with a party for which his housekeeper baked a cake. These parties, apparently given so extemporaneously, occupied more of his attention than he would have admitted; he was continually planning for them, telling people about them. Then there was another ritual of his office which took place every afternoon at five o'clock: at that hour he and his more important employees would go up to the dining room and have a drink.

In his apartment at Eighty-second Street and Park Avenue he entertains more formally. His wife, who was Mrs. Hugh Cabot, presides over dinners that are really dinner parties in the old-fashioned meaning of the term; the guests wear white ties and conversation is considered, and actually made to be, a sufficient means of entertainment. During the summer he takes Mrs. Ames and the children to North Easton, Massachusetts, where he spends most of his time gardening. Other things that interest him in addition to the theater are music and drawing plans for houses that he talks about building but never does. He is particularly fond of drawing bathhouses and hunting lodges. He has also invented a fictitious hobby to describe to people who ask him what his hobby is. He says that he has a mania for picking up pins—that he walks down the street looking for them, and when he sees one struggles vainly against the temptation to get hold of it. He elaborates this with the statement that his mania ceases to dominate him only when he goes into a dressmaking shop where pins are plentiful. Telling this story fills him with a glee which he seldom manages to conceal successfully. He has never picked up a pin in his life.

Only one thing about being a producer displeased him, and that was the necessity of letting the public know his plans. Often he did not announce that he was going to put on a play until the scenery had been built and the cast hired and set at work. Once a press agent convinced him that like other producers he ought to announce in the fall a list of the plays he was going to present that season; next day Ames handed him the list, which consisted of two plays. When his adviser objected that this would need padding, Ames agreed to pad it himself. He spent a happy morning making up play titles that he thought would look well on the list. The first was *One, Two, Three, and Out She Goes;* another *The Broadway Shepherdess,* by R. Notman. He said that if he could conduct his business the way he wanted to he would hire a dummy president for sixty or seventy dollars a week—some fellow dignified enough to sit on committees and look well in a frock coat. He would have this president's picture in every room of his offices and in the lobbies of his theaters while he himself, as the president's secretary, ran the company.

Winthrop Ames has written one play, from which he gets about six hundred dollars a year in royalties. It is a play for children called *Snow White,* and its ostensible author is one Jessie Bram White. When letters come from amateur companies asking Miss White to lower the royalty fee, Ames answers them, signing the lady's name in a delicate hand. He has always wanted and still wants to write a play he thinks is good enough to put his own name to, but lacks courage to begin it; his whole life of work in the theater has apparently only increased his appreciation of its difficulties. This appreciation is what makes him falter; he is the victim of his high standards of a good taste that remains the strongest thing in his character, stronger than his will, stronger than

his impulse to create. No play seemed good enough
to put on; he kept to a schedule of two plays a year,
or one; or sometimes none at all. But when
a play had once been chosen the whole routine
of his life, and even his personality, altered; his
critical activity swung with impressive energy into
construction; he drove his cast hard and himself
harder, attending personally to details of staging,
designing sets and occasionally even costumes. No
play ever satisfied him in its completed effect, but
during the period of preparation his social and
artistic abilities, usually unrelated, came nearest to
merging. Oddly enough, at the height of his work
as a producer his qualities as a Back Bay gentleman
most clearly proved their value.

By his tact he was able to keep a high-strung,
overwrought cast in a good humor longer and get
more work out of them than any other manager in
Broadway. Authors, composers, and specialists of
all sorts whose contracts are not regulated by Equity,
have been known to work for him without any contracts at all, knowing he considered himself bound
by arrangements made in a talk on the telephone or
a penciled memo. He was a producer who didn't get
sore at rehearsals, who treated humble people with
consideration, whom actors never had to sue to collect their salaries. On everything he did he set the

cold, polished seal of his courtesy, a courtesy that is the active complement of that negative quality here defined as taste. Its exercise gives him a way—perhaps the only way possible to him—of perfect artistic expression.

THE GREAT IMPERSONATION

THE GREAT IMPERSONATION

A STUDY OF DAVID BELASCO AT
SEVENTY-ONE

DAVID BELASCO has created one rôle that is undoubtedly immortal. It is the rôle of Belasco, the great producer. He has spent his life perfecting it, has built up a tradition to go with it, and for fifty years has dressed for it in a costume which he does not find less suitable because it happens also to be the official costume of ministers of the Gospel. In his old age his rôle has not failed him, and his days are still charged with histrionic intensity—brief contractions of disappointment, and expansive, contagious moments of triumph. There have been drawbacks to the maintenance of this rôle. Since the events of real life lack the consistency which an author puts in a play, a certain amount of effort has been needed to keep the rôle going, but nothing ever interrupted it. The rôle became a tradition which, renewed amazingly through three generations, has absorbed and partly concealed the stormy and immensely life-hungry and magnetic little man who has created it.

Ignoring for a minute this complication of Belasco's character, it will be simpler to consider what he has done. He is now seventy-one. He has been in the theatrical business since he was sixteen and a producer since he was twenty-one. In that time he has produced three hundred and seventy-four plays, counting *Dancing Partner*. You will understand how far back he goes in theatrical history when you realize that he is given credit for being the first producer to make footlights invisible to the audience by sinking them below the level of the stage. In his early days he originated many methods of stage lighting and scene manipulation that are still followed. Most important of all, he made his name connote a certain elementary realism in the theater— real books on the shelves of the stage library and real roses on the table beside the heroine's bed. People who, like him, feel the necessity of rooting make-believe in plainest reality take satisfaction in the knowledge that those parts of his stage stairways that you can't see from the orchestra are faithfully equipped with polished steps and a mahogany rail; one play that he put on acquired considerable advertisement from the fact that a letter brought on the stage by a courier as coming from a character familiar in history was the original manuscript of a letter written by that character.

Naturally such devices are inspired by smart

showmanship rather than by any thought of what their effect will be on the audience. Probably the greatest showman since Barnum, Belasco demands the same literalness from his casts as from his stage designers. He has crafty methods of getting it. A famous story concerns how he stuck a pin in Frances Starr. In rehearsing a scene requiring a scream, she had lifted her voice repeatedly without producing anything that sounded right. After screaming several times himself to show her how, Belasco told her to run off that part of the scene again. The male lead read his line once more, and Miss Starr screamed. It was no delicate shaded soprano sound, but full-throated, piercing. It was a scream. As she uttered it Miss Starr jumped slightly into the air and spun around, pressing one hand against the lower, rear portion of her dress. Belasco, who had been standing behind her, dropped the safety pin he had used in the interests of art, and soothed her, patting her hand, repeating, "That's it, that's it. Never forget how to do it."

He works furiously to get the effects he wants and is extremely sensitive to what people think of them. When he was rehearsing Ina Claire in a scene laid in an architect's office, he asked her what she thought of the stage set and seemed amazed to find that she was not enthusiastic.

"Why don't you like it?" he demanded.

Miss Claire said she knew an architect who had told her the set did not look the way an architect's office should. She related this lightly, while Belasco began to tremble. Everyone on the stage stared at him, feeling that something dramatic and perhaps terrible was about to happen. They were not disappointed. The producer ran to the wings and came back with a red fire ax. The appalled conclusion of the bystanders that Ina Claire had spoken her last line ended when Belasco turned away from her and hacked at the set. Repeating, "So you don't like it, so you don't like it, eh?" he swung the ax hard until he had broken up a good deal of the scenery that had taken weeks to build. Next day the carpenters began to build a new set under the supervision of an architect he called in as adviser.

Explaining the way he feels about the plays he puts on, he says, "I am a mother at heart," a statement which, like his writings, has more accuracy than its phraseology would seem to indicate. His sensitiveness, roused by any circumstance out of the ordinary, showed itself in typical fashion one night in Washington when a storm of applause interrupted the first act of a play he was presenting there.

"Do you hear it?" he whispered solemnly. "That is the greatest ovation I have ever received."

A few minutes later he found that the applause had been for President Wilson, who had come in late.

"What business has he coming here like that?" he said with annoyance.

At the end of the second act he took a curtain call himself. Receiving an even more enthusiastic reception than Wilson, he forgave the President for being tardy and often spoke of him after that with patriotic admiration.

During rehearsals he does more acting than any member of his cast. In any situation he can be depended on for a histrionic response. Anyone who mentions money to him while he is working precipitates an immediate rage, as when a young actor who had been promoted from an obscure to a better part in *Lulu Belle* chose a time when the whole company was on the stage to ask him for a raise.

"Get out of here," yelled Belasco. "Get out of here before I knock you down and trample on your dirty face. Throw him out," he shouted as the actor began to slink toward the wings. "He wants money, does he? Kick him! Why, I wouldn't let anyone do that to me. I wouldn't let the author himself come in here now and ask and make demands for money."

Patently this speech was aimed less at the real offender than at Charles MacArthur with whom he had quarreled that morning about some detail in the manuscript and who was sitting at the moment within easy reach of his voice. He fights with most of his authors but makes up with them again. Whether or not they think he improves their plays by the changes he insists on, they generally speak of him afterward with a kind of warmth and delight in an effort to make others understand that working with him and perhaps even quarreling with him was a rich and worthwhile experience.

Sometimes his abstractions or rages are unquestionably assumed for avoiding disagreeable situations. Actors who have worked for him state their suspicion that, although when approached on the subject of salary he asserts obscurely that they will have to see his casting director, he picks up his telephone in the studio while they are going downstairs and names a figure to the executives in the office below. When the stage carpenters working on the sets for *Mima* threatened to knock off unless he paid them several thousand dollars owing in back pay, he made an appeal to them, suggesting that artists at work on something beautiful should be superior to mercenary considerations. His address,

though persuasive, did not move the union carpenters, and he had to send to the bank for cash.

His disregard of production costs is part of his
instinct for dramatizing what he does; he sees himself as one of those managers who shout to his
subordinates, "Get that no matter what it costs."
This is a pose that suits his nature; he is generous,
impulsive, and a bad business man; the ardor he
applies to producing plays is an enthusiast's ardor,
and the huge investments he sometimes puts into
them, such as spending three hundred thousand
dollars for the ironwork in *Mima,* are not made
primarily in the hope of financial profits but because
of his belief in the value of what he is doing. He
keeps most of his plays in rehearsal five or six
weeks, although the usual period is two or three.
Sometimes just before an opening night he decides
that the company isn't ready yet and rehearses them
a couple of weeks more or takes them on the road.
He uses bigger casts than most producers, sticking
to his theory that a stage crowd ought to look like a
crowd; he pays his supers top wages. Usually, in addition to what is required by contract, he gives them
a dollar a day for lunch during rehearsal. When
he was producing *The Merchant of Venice,* on which
he lost a quarter of a million, he sent people to
Venice to study settings and costume, and paid

forty thousand dollars for Portia's costumes alone. He kept *Fanny* on Broadway for weeks after it should normally have closed, losing four or five thousand a week on it because he insisted that Fanny Brice was a great actress and that the play was going to be a hit.

Critics often express amazement at the money he will put into some more or less tawdry production, finding it hard to understand why a producer whose plays seem aimed at the box office should stage them with a splendor quite unnecessary and likely to do away with his profits. Other people have been so impressed with his long list of successes that they give him credit for being a shrewd judge of popular taste. The truth is that Belasco does not aim at the box office and isn't shrewd in the least. He puts on plays that he likes as effectively as he can and does well at it because his taste, naïve and essentially theatrical, happens also to be the taste of thousands of other people. At handling the mechanical problems of the theater he is ingenuous, but no less so with his private affairs; even at the best of times never gets much saved up. When he has money to spare he buys a lot of antiques and when he hasn't he buys them anyway and charges them till he puts on another hit. Elephants of all sizes, made of ivory, ebony, jade, or porcelain, appeal to him strongly;

battalions of them march across the tables of his comfortable four-room apartment on the fifth floor of the Gladstone; one room is furnished with gilt, brocaded chairs of the First Empire on which nobody is allowed to sit. He owns the most complete dramatic library in the country and a collection of Napoleonic relics that is very valuable. He has never bought a bond, traded in the market, or worn jewelry except a plain gold ring presented to him long ago by one of his elocution classes. Antiques are his only investments. He sold some of them to produce *The Bachelor Father,* his first success after a series of failures.

Most of his things are in the studio on the third floor of the Belasco Theater. You go in through the stage door and up a private elevator into a room filled with glassware, then into the room where he has the Napoleonic stuff, including a lock of Napoleon's hair with a letter to prove it is genuine, then through the library and an indoor garden and a little room decorated only with a crucifix. There is an atmosphere of whispers, magnificence, and stealthy footsteps; you feel that secret panels are opening and closing behind the tapestries and that each suit of armor probably contains a living body.

Belasco's office is the last of seven connecting rooms. It is furnished with historic relics. His waste-paper basket is made out of a drum that the Germans used at the siege of Paris in 'seventy-two, and the tiles in his fireplace are said to have been stolen two hundred years ago out of the Alhambra at Granada. Somehow these things are appropriate to him, like his black patent-leather boots with long points and buttoned tops, and his blue shirts and flat black ties, broad enough to cover the little notch at the top of his high waistcoats, and the high round collars which he has had made to order for fifty years and which he insists are not a priest's collars because they have a minute opening in the center. All this sort of thing is part of the unique atmosphere he has created around himself, an atmosphere derived from the theater, from its modes and gestures adapted to his personality through a career as astonishing as a drawing-room melodrama of the 'nineties.

II

When a play doesn't go well Belasco puts down its failure to the cabals of people leagued against him. "I have enemies," he whispers, shaking his shaggy white head and sweeping his hand away from his chest in a dramatic gesture. What is this world delightful of fantasy that he makes real to you— intrigue and pomp with him the center of it all? Even in his appearance there is something suggestive of fairy story—his short, bent, robust, big-boned body, with its forward-pointing shoulders and big head. His hair is thick, silky, and glistening white, and in a point on his forehead hangs the lock which for fifty years, with a characteristic motion of his hand, he has brushed back at the moment when he came out to take a curtain call at first performances.

When called out, it is a habit of his to say a few words to the audience. His language then is grave and measured, but in private he talks rapidly in a low tone, almost whispering, accentuating words beginning with s; his sentences trail into each other, and he begins a new one while the pantomime of his hands and face fills up the meaning of the one he left unfinished. This pattern is made still more complicated by his method of talking in abstract quantities, avoiding whenever possible mentioning a definite event or a person's name, but referring instead to "a certain person" or "an unfortunate incident." Sometimes emotion wakens as he remembers things long past, and then the words come out in a flood, fast and orderly. All his vitality seems concentrated in his brown eyes, which have the look of vivid youth peculiar to the eyes of very healthy old men. His face, ruggedly made, is furrowed with deep lines in the cheeks and around the mouth. His pretentions to vast energy are not a pose. The company rehearsing *Mima* was driven through a sixteen-hour dress rehearsal by an old gentleman with blazing eyes who assured them in momentary pauses that they would have a day's rest before the opening. He meant the day between breakfast and the curtain of the first performance at eight-thirty that evening.

Sometimes he deliberately exaggerates the accounts of his feats of endurance. He tells with a kind of mischievous pride how long he has been working, and his daughter, Mrs. Morris Gest, coming up to see him in the late afternoon or evening, reproves him, as he expects her to, perhaps tells him to go to bed. They compromise by going for a drive in the automobile he doesn't own but has rented so long it seems as though it belonged to him. This drive up Riverside or along Fifth Avenue is the only recreation he takes. He lives by himself; all his relatives are dead except Mrs. Gest. He had another daughter who died as a child and is buried in a tomb in a Brooklyn cemetery where a light is kept burning all the time because she used to be afraid in the dark. His wife died a little while ago. They had lived apart for years before her death, but they were never separated in any legal or even human sense. He was rehearsing *Lulu Belle* when she died, and for several nights in succession sat up all night beside her bed. In the morning, after half an hour's sleep, he went down to work as usual.

Outside of his family, the most important influence in Belasco's life is a woman who has never been on the stage and who holds a rather low opinion of it as a serious profession. Her name is Elizabeth Ginty. She used to be his secretary, but she came in time to be a sort of manager and housekeeper, correcting manuscripts with him, planning his meals, and making suggestions about the theater. She has her own house and her own cook now, but she still prepares everything he eats and sends it over to the Gladstone or his studio in an asbestos hamper. Miss Ginty is an intelligent woman, and it has been rumored that her share in shaping the plays he wrote went much farther than taking them down in shorthand. Once long ago someone found them on their hands and knees in Belasco's studio picking up and piecing together scraps of the only existing copy of *Madame Butterfly* which they had torn up in an argument. Elizabeth Ginty was a great friend of Mrs. Belasco and the two women conspired to make things go the way they wanted. In Belasco's life, a hurly-burly involving most people who entered it with some extreme of adulation or enmity directed toward him, Elizabeth Ginty stands as the warm human embodiment of common sense and proper behavior.

Luck, even to the fortunate, rarely vouchsafes more than one Ginty in a lifetime, yet there are a number of people who have dedicated themselves with amazing disinterestedness to Belasco's affairs. There is a fellow named Curry, a conservative middle-aged man with a slow voice and a photographic memory, whose official title is private secretary but who performs numberless functions unusual for secretaries. He arrives at the Gladstone when Belasco gets up at half-past seven or eight and accompanies him until he goes to bed at two or three; Curry's is the voice that answers you when you telephone D. B., as his staff calls him; it is Curry who sees that the right manuscripts are taken from the hotel to the studio, who tells D. B. when it is time to eat and if necessary heats and serves the food Miss Ginty has sent over, who runs errands, writes letters, acts as valet if D. B. is doing without a valet, and nurses him if he has a cold or is suffering from one of his headaches. And there are other Gintys: Belasco's bookkeeper, his chief electrician, his casting director—all highly efficient in their fields, could make more money somewhere else, but stay with him year after year, held by some illusive quality in him which asserts at all times his right to be taken care of.

From such associates, considering their earnest viewpoint and their unrivaled opportunities for documentation, you would expect a mass of testimony on their master's career. Curiously enough, perhaps because of its duration, D. B.'s story, particularly its beginnings, remains somewhat vague. About ten years ago it was all incorporated in a two-volume biography by William Winter, which is good reading if you have time for it, but not to be compared to Belasco's verbal narration of the same material. He goes far back, to the beginning, in fact, of European history—mentions floods, invasions, plagues, leading up to the migration of his father, "the first Harlequin of London," and his mother, sprung from an old Spanish line, to California in 1848. His own birth, taking place in a cellar, is not without its Biblical suggestions, and he relates how after obtaining his early education in a monastery he joined a circus, where he was tossed through burning hoops from the back of a galloping horse.

Disengaging the facts from this æneid is a ticklish business. He was born in 1859. That has been established. It is also positive that his father, "the

first Harlequin of London," was a clown who quit
his profession in 1849 to look for gold but didn't
have much luck. For a while David was a super in
the California Theater in San Francisco and afterward wrote plays and arranged stage effects for the
Baldwin Theater. It is hard to discover anything
relevant to the monastic period of his early life.
Since his father was a Hebrew, David's connection
with the Roman Catholic Church must have been
even more nebulous than he suggests. Certainly, in
some way religious costumes took hold of his
imagination and have influenced his whole life. There
is no doubt that his collar and tie are meant to suggest a clergyman's dress, and various examples of
religious realism, notably the crucifix, attract him
deeply. In his apartment in the Gladstone there is a
closet that has been made into an exact replica of a
Catholic high altar. He shows this closet to visitors,
hinting at a mystery, and then—with sudden effect—
opening the closet door. The little shrine is beautiful,
but sometimes his triumph is impaired by some de-
fect in the mechanism adjusted to the hinges of the
door, and he shakes his head, murmuring gently
and mournfully, as though to himself, "The bells
ought to be ringing. The bells ought to be ringing."

He left San Francisco several times to go on tour
with road companies, occasions when he added to

his wages by peddling a patent medicine in country towns. This medicine was a gargle his mother used to put up. He usually got stranded somewhere and bummed his way back to San Francisco. He wasn't a good actor. His face, unusually handsome in repose, became contorted when he tried to express emotion. He did better with his writing: several of his plays, especially *La Belle Russe,* were hits on the West Coast. He was stage manager of three San Francisco theaters when he left in 1882 and came East. He arranged lighting effects at the Madison Square Theater for twenty-five dollars a week. Here he got the idea of setting the gas footlights below the level of the stage, hiding them under a metal hood. He wrote more plays, and the Madison Square Theater performed some of them successfully; his royalty was fifteen dollars a performance. The town's first speculators got five dollars a seat for his smash hit *May Blossoms.* Before long he got a new job as stage manager and stock dramatist of the old Lyceum Theater on Fourth Avenue. In his spare time he trained society girls who wanted to act, coaching their plays and teaching them elocution; it was his reputation for this sort of thing that led to his meeting Mrs. Leslie Carter whom he made into the greatest American actress of her period.

III

What preceded Mrs. Carter's career on the stage invokes the atmosphere of the old Sunday supplements where that part of her story is buried and half-forgotten. It invokes a lost generation, actualities that have faded from the florid sketches bordering the test—the men in square-shouldered coats buttoning high in front—the arabesque motif of dollar signs and wineglasses and Mrs. Carter turning her tiny waist to look over her shoulder with shadowy allurement. She was a Kentucky girl who before she was twenty left a family of horse-riding brothers and cousins to marry the elderly and distinguished manufacturer of Carter's Little Liver Pills. That she found life dismal in her husband's big house was established a few years later in the most sensational divorce case ever publicly tried in Chicago. When she met Belasco the trial was still going on. She had come to New York during an adjournment of the court with her mind made up to find some way of supporting herself after she had suffered the disgrace the pill manufacturer was so effectively arranging. In those days notoriety was not as salable as it is now. Mrs. Carter thought that with a little training she could be an actress. Belasco, talking to her, was not so sure.

"What kind of a play do you want?"

She laughed. "I can ride well. Give me a racing play—I'll come on riding."

A producer who had been looking for beauty alone would have been disappointed. That, certainly, was not the charm of this elegant, moody woman, with her red hair, prominent nose, and deliberate, rather affected voice. She went back to Chicago, but a little later came East again and had an interview with Belasco at Echo Lake, where he was working on a play. She told him the story of her life, and as he listened to her passionate words, watching her as she moved around a hotel room, he realized that she had the qualities of a great actress. His first idea was to put her in something at the Lyceum. When the directors refused to consider this, asking him to resign if he continued plans for her, he gave up his job and began rehearsing her in *The Ugly Duckling*.

Belasco put on the play with money personally guaranteed and later collected by lawsuit from a rich man who had known Mrs. Carter before her divorce. While they were rehearsing in New York, she lived in a furnished room in the Bowery, selling her dresses and jewels to buy meals. Although she had never studied acting before, her anxiety to do well as a means of wiping out the experience she had just been through gave her a tremendous capacity for work. Newspapers were suggesting that if the play included Chicago in its tour the people from the big houses on the lakeside would come down to the theater and throw eggs. Belasco saw the value of taking this risk. If she failed in a hostile town, Mrs. Carter might still go over in other cities; while if she was a success, there would be nothing more to worry about anywhere.

There were some boos as she stepped on the stage. She was very pale, and her voice was uneven. At the end of the first act the audience became quiet, and at the end of the second they stood up and cheered. For the next fifteen years Mrs. Carter was the most important woman on the American stage. When she played *Zaza* in London, Edward, Prince of Wales, went to see her six times. Before the play was over he would usually be weeping with sentimental dignity in the royal box because, as he explained, she reminded him of a lost sweetheart. Always Mrs. Carter appeared in Belasco's productions until one day she ran away and got married. Belasco has never seen her since. He used to refuse to speak of her, saying dramatically that he had "closed the iron door." Sometimes he forgets this and talks about her with great charm. Mrs. Carter herself, old now, trouping occasionally with a stock company, or on a mean vaudeville circuit, likes to say that she and Belasco are reconciled—that they are going to put on a play together the way they did in the old days.

Mrs. Carter was the first of a long succession of actors and actresses that he developed. David Warfield, famous in Weber and Fields shows, had played nothing but comedy parts with a beard and a funny nose when Belasco gave him his first straight rôle. When someone brought a precocious, golden-haired girl named Gladys Smith to recite for him he put her in one of his shows and helped her think up the new and more engaging name of Mary Pickford. He took a special interest in another little girl named Blanche Bates because he had acted with her mother, and he had promised Mrs. Bates that if possible he would make an actress out of Blanche. Frances Starr was standing on a chair watching a hypothetical horse run in a stock company play about racing when he first saw her. Impressed by the way she used her face and hands, he went backstage and put her on contract. He found Leo Dietrichstein playing in the German theater on Irving Place and promised him a part if he would learn English. Dietrichstein's father ran a little hotel on Fourth Avenue. Lenore Ulric came to the Belasco Theater in answer to an advertisement calling for supers; she was sick and out of a job. After watching her at rehearsals he took her out of the show but kept her on his payroll until she was well enough to be trained for a better part. Ina Claire had done nothing more impressive than imitations in musical shows when he began to train her. He likes to poke around in shoddy halls and settlement theaters looking for talent. When one generation of stage people becomes too eminent to be submissive to directing, he starts developing a new one.

His ability to find new stars has never been equaled by his cleverest competitors. It is unfortunately far more emphatic than his understanding on the literary side of plays. The best of those he wrote himself—*Madame Butterfly, The Darling of the Gods, The Return of Peter Grimm*—were extraordinarily successful theatrically, far above the standards of their time and good enough to hold their own in technical respects with most plays written long after them. Those he produced without having helped to write were chosen because they had much the same qualities of theatrical effectiveness. Plays which obtain their effects by poetry or implication bore and puzzle him, and when they have good runs he cannot understand it, usually attributing their success to bribery of critics by the producer. In his catalogue of productions—a list so long that it has been bound into a pretty book with a flower as the cover design—there are no plays by Barrie, Shaw, Galsworthy, O'Neill or any of the other authors accepted in contemporary circles as belonging to the first rank. But the plays on that list have satisfied the idea of what "going to the theater" meant to two and a half generations of Americans—plays which have been skillfully and vividly staged, which have influenced fashions, introduced catchwords, been important in the topical history of their times. No Shaw or Galsworthy or O'Neill, but Belasco. His own authors have found that whether they liked it or not there was as much of Belasco as themselves in their work by the time the dress rehearsal was over.

At home early last summer he spent most of his time in his bedroom, wearing pajamas and a sky-blue dressing gown and using a card table for a desk. Here he read plays, interviewed actors, and talked to technicians. His doctor had him on a diet, but once in a while he would order up the rich foods he wanted, saying that what the doctor didn't know wouldn't hurt him. He likes benedictine and fruit compotes; if anyone dining with him doesn't eat his compote, Belasco is apt to jump up and put it on the window ledge to have later himself. The only thing that interferes with his delight in life is the suggestion that it is time for him to retire. If you say anything about that he gets so angry that he trembles all over. In his blue robe, with his fluffy white hair rumpled and his lined, big-featured face twisting with rage, he defies a swarm of enemies whom he does not identify. "I wish I knew who started all that talk," he cries. "I'm sick and tired of it. Just because they are old and decrepit and played out, they think I am. But I'm stronger than I've ever been in my life. If I could tell who started all that talk I'd hit him on the nose. I'm a dignified man, but I would hit him on the nose and turn him around and kick him around the town. I'll be working when they are in jail or rotting in their graves."

ALL THE KING'S HORSES

ALL THE KING'S HORSES

LIKE all trainers of racehorses, the late Samuel Hildreth was an expert in the physical culture of animals, and a kind of impresario as well. He was an interesting, rather eccentric fellow himself; many stories are told about the great races his horses won, the way he behaved at the track, his superstitions, and his methods of training, but the important thing about him remained his ability to tell what a horse would do from indications often subtle and obscure. Many people think they can judge horses like that, but none of them around here has proved it to the extent that he did.

He was a broad-shouldered, white-haired gentleman, with glossy, nervous brown eyes, and a clear, tough-looking skin that was sunburned all the year round. Everything about him seemed to have been made to last: his knob-like cheekbones made his face look square, and the rest of his body was warmly covered, even in summer, with various thick, protective layers of clothing. His overcoats were squarely cut, and had exceptionally big buttons; his shoes were heavy; he always wore a waistcoat and a big watch-chain, and his short, white mustache covered his mouth like a flap over a pocket. That mustache was symbolic in a way, for he was very close-mouthed. He rarely talked about the horses he trained, and regarded with suspicion any stranger introduced to him at the track. On exceptional occasions, or when in the company of old friends, he would let out what he thought of the field that day, circling with a pencil mark the entries he liked in each race. He marked Harry F. Sinclair's program this way when E. E. Smathers, whose stable he had trained, introduced the oil magnate as "a baseball fan who is just finding out about racing." Sinclair, profiting by his tips, got interested enough to buy a share in one horse, then in several others that Hildreth owned and was racing at the time under his own colors. Together they bought and started to renovate Rancocas, the stud farm Pierre Lorillard had built at Jobstown, New Jersey. Eventually the venture became so big that Hildreth sold out his interest to Sinclair and changed his position from part owner to trainer and general manager at a salary and share in the winnings.

Until his death he continued to train for Rancocas and raced the stable while his employer was in jail. Even when the oil man was at the track every day Hildreth decided the policy of the stable—what horses were to be bought, which sold, which run, which scratched—and Sinclair indorsed his decisions almost without exception. As the directing authority of Rancocas, he achieved the greatest success of his life, but he was successful and well known long before he met Sinclair. He raced and trained horses with more or less good luck for about fifty years.

He was born in Independence, Missouri, in 1866; his father was a tobacco planter who paid attention to his plantation only when his quarter-horses were not making money. When his children were still small, Vincent Hildreth lost interest in tobacco altogether and, with his furniture packed into four wagons, and ten or twelve racers and half-a-dozen hackneys in a line behind them, left Missouri and went to Kansas and then to Kentucky and Texas, looking for race meets. Young Sam began his professional activity trading a mule for a pony and the pony for a gelding, which his father sold at a profit. Later he rode in some races. Sometimes he spoke of them, referring laconically to a fabulous number of victories.

These races aren't in the record books. They were run on little prairie tracks in Texas—the last of them in Dallas, when, at sixteen, he was picking up too much weight to be a jockey. He trained some horses for a man named Paris, who was proprietor of the

Belmont Hotel in Parsons, Kansas. Besides being trainer, Hildreth was clerk and bartender in the hotel and did odd jobs. At twenty-two he learned blacksmithing and appeared at some of the Eastern tracks, making racing plates in partnership with a German named Long. He earned enough to buy a cheap horse of his own, then another one; trading his bargains for better horses, or improving them by training, he worked up to the big tracks. One year he won sixty races. To get a fair price for his entries, which were acquiring so much prestige that they were handicapped in the betting, he hired Frank James, brother of Jesse, to bet his money without letting the bookies know where it came from. He used to say that James was one of the most honest commissioners he ever knew.

After his marriage to a girl he met at Saratoga when he was twenty-six, he was flush and broke by turns for a number of years. Sometimes Mrs. Hildreth, who went to the track with him nearly every day during the season, had a hard time finding anything for supper. Once he had as much as fifty thousand dollars, but a few months later it was all gone. Penniless, he was hurt in a street-car accident. When he got out of the hospital the street-car company paid him five hundred dollars in damages. Hildreth bet the money on a horse. That his entry won does not keep you from wondering why his curious methods of arranging his financial affairs made him a millionaire while others who have run their lives on similar principles are now selling gum and programs at the track.

What made him rich is undoubtedly the fact that his gambling—and he bet more often and in bigger amounts than was commonly supposed—was only a side issue of the training for which he paid high wages and which exercised his real genius. Lucky Baldwin was the first owner who persuaded him to give up his independence and insecurity by becoming trainer for a big private stable. After Baldwin, he trained for William C. Whitney, August Belmont, Charles E. Kohler, E. E. Smathers, and others. Almost all the famous sporting figures of a decade or two ago were friends of his: "Betcha-a-Million" Gates and Diamond Jim Brady, who would yell and jump around when his horses were running, and Pittsburgh Phil Smith, who never let out a sound; Bill Pinkerton, who, when he was putting a big bet down, would have the detectives of his agency distribute it all over the country so as not to hurt the odds. Owners like Eugene Leigh and the Baron Maurice Rothschild, jockeys like Carroll Shilling and Snapper Garrison, and Tod Sloan, who traveled with twenty trunks full of clothes and who out of conceit always registered in hotels as James Sloan, of New York City, although he came from Kokomo, Indiana. Hildreth trained such horses as Hourless, Mad Play, Stromboli, Silver Fox, Superlette, Nedaña, and Grey Lag. In four years Rancocas won a total of one million, two hundred thousand dollars in purses. Zev alone brought in more than three hundred thousand dollars.

Although horses that he trained have won, at some time or another, virtually every important racing fixture in the country, he only took the Kentucky Derby once—with Zev, in 1923. He seldom trained for one particular race, preferring to concentrate on the ordinary day-to-day events at the track, finding or creating some situation that would be an advantage to his entry. One funny part of his system was the way he kept his stable fat. When the horses were led down to the track to be exercised early in the morning he would look them over and send some back to the barn; these were the ones he thought looked in racing condition. Most other trainers exercise even the horses that are ready to do their best; in fact, if any other trainer sent an entry to the post as fat as some of Hildreth's horses were, no one would believe that it was fit. Because he kept flesh on them, his horses lasted longer and were able to retain top form with only short lay-

offs during an entire season. Knowing that he would
not be expected to have anything fast before the
weather was warm, he arrived at the Jamaica opening one spring with twenty two-year-olds which he
said were "nothing much." In the first two weeks
of racing he had one or more winners every day, and
in a number of races where he entered two horses
they finished first and second. Friends who had believed him when he called the two-year-olds indif-
ferent were indignant at being kept out of his
confidence, but he had told them the truth. After the
first two weeks other horses rounded into shape and
his average of winning went down. His two-year-
olds were not exceptionally fast, but had cleaned up
because, by a trick of training, he had brought them
down from the farm ready to do their best.

Several anecdotes illustrate his shrewdness in
turning accidents to his advantage. A Rancocas horse
named Cheops, being led out for saddling, knocked
off a racing plate by stubbing his toe on a plank
in the paddock gateway. Hildreth sent for a farrier
and while waiting had a stable boy lead Cheops
slowly up and down the paddock. A few minutes later
the rumor that Cheops was lame, reaching the enclosure, created excitement and alarm. The horse
was a favorite at odds-on.

"Go out and see for yourself," insisted a pale young man who had brought the news.

Betters hurried to the paddock, where they saw Cheops moving around unevenly on his three shoes.

"Did he bow a tendon?" somebody asked.

Although the boy said nothing, his silence apparently confirmed the idea that the horse was hopelessly crippled. In spite of Hildreth's reputation for running his entries only when they were fit, the odds on Cheops lengthened fast and were long enough to be profitable by the time a farrier got a new plate on him. Presumably with some money down at the new price, Hildreth watched him win the race with ease.

Profiting by an incident like this wasn't deliberate slyness on his part as much as wit in turning whatever happened to his own account. He never told anybody how much he had down on horses he liked, but from the effect of his bets on the odds in the enclosure it has been deduced that he occasionally went as high as twenty thousand in a single race. His salary was reputed to be a hundred thousand a year.

Occasionally he showed a sentimental attachment for a horse that had done well for him. He said that Grey Lag, a handsome chestnut with a white belly and white legs, was the most intelligent animal he ever trained. Stromboli was another he liked a lot. After buying him for a trifling price at the end of his racing career he got the idea that maybe Stromboli wasn't too old to race after all. Instead of using him for a saddle horse, as he had planned at first, he began to train him, and two years after his first retirement entered him at a mile race at Belmont with horses that hadn't even been foaled when he was at the top of his career. Stromboli won the race and another as well before Hildreth retired him for good.

Green and white are the colors of the Rancocas stable; they are also the colors painted brightly on the gas pumps of Sinclair filling stations along highways. Like the oil company, the big stable at Jobstown is organized on an expensive scale. A thousand acres are sown in grass for racehorses to graze on; the low-roofed building containing the stalls is nearly a quarter of a mile long. Besides the regular outdoor running tracks there is an indoor track—until recently the only one in the United States—enclosed entirely in glass. Thoroughbreds training in the transparent, oval building in the wintertime look like equine figures in a merry-go-round, whirling at startling speed to the music of an inaudible calliope.

Training goes on at Jobstown nine months a year. Hildreth spent this period quietly in a modest house on the stable estate. He used to get up every morn-

ing at four-thirty to see his horses exercised, but an
illness that preceded the one that caused his death
made him careful of his health—kept him from being quite as active as he had been. During the summer
he traveled around the circuit with the Rancocas entries, usually renting a cottage near whatever track
they were racing on. What he did in his spare time,
and what amusements, if any, he enjoyed other than
racing, few people knew. Horses were apparently his
hobby as well as his profession. He was seldom seen
anywhere except at the track, rarely went to the
theater, and avoided big hotels. The only unpro-
fessional interest he frankly revealed was in children. He had none himself, but when he met a
friend who had he rarely failed to inquire in sporting terms about their health. "How're the fillies?"

Possibly his unwillingness to talk about his own
horses was not owing as much to taciturnity as to
some superstition. His life was complicated with
dozens of taboos, charms, and rituals. Besides the
common distrust of black cats, two-dollar bills, and
the number thirteen, he superstitiously avoided
cross-eyed people and would not have a gray horse
in his stable. Silver Fox, which raced with distinction in the Rancocas silks, was purchased by
Mrs. Sinclair over his protest. He believed that dogs,
especially small ones with long hair, brought luck,

and when possible secured his lucky dogs in pairs so as to breed them and renew his luck through successive generations. He would not travel himself or let any of his horses travel on Friday. Once he shipped several entries to Pimlico on a Thursday, believing that they would get there at six or seven the same evening. Something happened that kept the horses from arriving punctually. It was exercise time on Friday morning before Hildreth found that they had come.

"What time last night did these horses get in?"

Told that it had not been until a little after one in the morning, he chewed his mustache for a minute, then flourished an arm. "All right, pack them up to-morrow. We're going to Bowie."

One of his superstitions concerned the spot in the paddock at Belmont where his horses were brought to be saddled. Every stable has by tradition some special saddling place. Hildreth's was under a tall, lopsided tamarack on the west side of the wide lawn, near the driveway going up to the stands. He usually saddled all Rancocas entries himself. First the stable-boy handed him a linen towel lettered with the name of the jockey who had the leg up; the trainer laid the towel on the horse's back, smoothing it so that all the hairs would lie one way. Over the towel came a thin sweat pad, then the leather bag containing the weights, then the saddlecloth with the entry's number on it, then the saddle pad. He put the saddle on and cinched it before strolling back to the clubhouse. He rarely gave riding instructions to Laverne Fator, who during Earl Sande's temporary retirement did most of the riding for Rancocas. It was a saying at the track that Fator was the best horse in Hildreth's barn.

His habit of making a superstitious ritual out of saddling caused some confusion before one of the most important races ever run at Belmont—the match between Zev and Papyrus in 1923. Zev had won the Kentucky Derby, Papyrus the English Derby. Steve Donoghue, the smartest jockey in England, was riding against Earl Sande, and the race had been publicized as "The International Derby." The stableboy had just taken the blanket off Zev so that Hildreth could saddle him when an official came along and said that a special enclosure had been built to saddle the two horses in.

"It's a rare occasion," the official explained. "You see, the crowd is so big that the Association thought it would be better——"

The trainer cut him short.

"What do you think I want to do," he demanded with suppressed fury, "change my luck?"

Papyrus alone was saddled in the special enclosure. As the horses went to the post Hildreth saw Basil Jarvis, who had trained the English horse, milling in the crowd for a place to stand. Reaching a hand down, he pulled up the Englishman, and the two trainers watched the race from the same box. Hildreth had trained other great horses, but none as fast as Zev; though Papyrus was under the handicap of being away from home, it was a creditable and important race to win. Zev took an early lead and, coming into the stretch, pulled a little farther away from Papyrus. Jarvis turned and congratulated Hildreth. The race was not over yet; it was still possible for Zev to stumble or slow up, or for Papyrus to pass him, but this did not happen. The Rancocas horse passed over the line five lengths in the lead with Sande looking over his shoulder to see where Papyrus was. The finish in the misty summer weather, with Zev in a white racing hood and Sande looking back, made a great scene; of all the races he won, the many changing scenes of crowds dark at the rail and horses going past the stands, that moment might be picked out, for some figurative quality, to stand for all the rest—galloping images for a medallion of excitement and romance.

THE EMERALD CHERUB

B OSS" is a good word—not a word native
to this language but one to which we have
given new corpulence. And here is a man
who is a boss—John H .McCooey, sixty-six years
old, Democratic Leader in Kings County, Brooklyn,
a county that has more votes in it than any other in
America. He is an almost perfect illustration of
what the word "boss" really means.

Think of an Irishman with a short nose, pale
eyes, and the sort of clear pallid skin that is achieved
only by babies and by old men who have lived successful lives. His mustache is long and white. There
is an old-world touch in that mustache, an accent
that is repeated in the solidity of his short thick
body, in the solitaire in his cravat, in his starched
formal cuffs, in his handkerchiefs, big as table-
cloths, with borders an inch wide. His voice is delicate and light; when you hear it on the telephone it
sounds like a boy's voice. And his face, in spite of its
thickness, its pallor, its bald crown, is very young.

Perhaps, out of all these details, you might fasten
on his voice as the most characteristic thing about
John McCooey. His mind is like his voice—wary,

light, sensitive, and young. That is why he gives you a new idea about the word "boss." Remembering Mr. Hanna and how he broke with Roosevelt; thinking of the late Mr. Murphy and of the methods by which he beat his way up from a free-lunch counter, people are apt to find in the word "boss" the boom of angry, unforgotten voices, the reek of cigars. That is a mistake. Mr. Hanna and Mr. Murphy were great political leaders not because of their lunge and swagger but because they had exactly the same quality that makes the voice of John McCooey wary and light.

A boss rarely bosses. He suggests. He deflects. He absorbs. A boss cannot hold an important official post without sacrificing the weight of his unofficial one. Mr. McCooey now holds no official city post. He used to be the clerk of the Surrogate Court, an office that carried a salary of $10,500 a year, but could not by itself account for his present reputation and affluence. A boss builds his house on a hill of packed-down handshakes. Only when a long time has passed, a time barren of any ponderable achievement, spent in listening, in smiling, and doing petty favors, is the foundation finished; and then political opponents find that a hill of feathers is harder to shake than a hill of stone.

To become a county leader, a man usually passes

through three positions—district captain, committeeman, district leader. These posts are political and
legal. They are not official. They have nothing to
do with government but only with the formation of
government—they are part of what is referred to,
with needless mystery, as the "machine," *i. e.,* a
party organization for choosing and supporting can-
didates for election. Each of the positions of captain, committeeman, and district leader lifts a man
forward into a personal and political influence that
is out of all proportion to the status of those cog-
wheel positions; the district leader who has the most
influence is apt to be chosen borough leader. He is
then unofficial Czar over the district leaders, the
committeemen, the captains; he decides who shall
hold all the other offices that his party controls in the
county. He is a boss. John McCooey has held this
position in Kings County for twenty years.

"How did you come to enter politics, Mr.
McCooey?" reporters ask him.

"Oh," he says, "naturally . . . you drift into
politics quite naturally."

A turn of his plump hand indicates the natural
process by which you drift into politics.

It is true that John McCooey drifted into politics.
But first a certain incident cut him away from his
anchorage. His father, an ironworker in Pennsyl-

vania, fell through a hatchway and was killed. John
McCooey, then thirteen, went to Brooklyn with his
mother and supported her by working as a pattern
maker in the Morgan Iron Works. In the evenings
he went to the local Democratic headquarters.

When he needed a new job his district captain
found one for him in the Brooklyn Navy Yard; then
a vacancy occurred in the Post Office Department
and Democratic friends got him appointed superintendent of Station S.

The story of this time would be a story of many
meetings, of introductions on street corners and in
committee rooms, of solemn banquets at which he
heard the leaders of his party express their assurances of fellowship and their anticipations of prosperity in the florid political English he has learned
to use so well. One night when he was closing up
the post office a man in a B. R. T. cap asked for a
money-order blank.

"White or pink?" demanded John McCooey. The
white were for domestic drafts, the pink foreign.
They were on a table by the window.

The man said he wanted a white one. He chatted
while he filled it out—seventy-five dollars for his
mother in Pennsylvania to pay the interest on a mort-
gage. He had saved the money, he said, out of his

wages as a subway motorman. He signed his name
—John F. Hylan.

Thus began a friendship that grew and solidified
while Hylan, the motorman, became successively a
lawyer, a county judge, and then, for two terms,
mayor. By the time Hylan announced that he would
stand for a third term Tammany had had enough of
him, and John McCooey, because of their friendship, was faced with a problem that he could not
solve by any of the familiar rules of boss-ship. There
was no fence to straddle: he had to declare himself.
Was he for Hylan or for Tammany? McCooey refused to answer as long as he could. Then he said he
was for Hylan.

You could find any number of motives for this
move. Perhaps it was sentiment—his loyalty for a
man who had fought the same battles, sprung from
the same background as himself; perhaps a stronger
motive was his ambition to assume the leadership of
Tammany, a position that would clearly be his if he
forced the election of Hylan over Tammany's veto.
Two boroughs—Manhattan and the Bronx—stood
with Tammany; two—Queens and Richmond—with
Hylan. McCooey was the keystone. His vote, as
leader of the fifth borough, would determine the
nomination. Any candidate he named, even if he

named himself, would have the support of Tammany —any candidate, that is, except Hylan. McCooey could not be budged. "Tammany shall not cross the bridge," he said.

He carried the fight into the primaries. Not that he had any objection to Mr. Walker—he did not know Mr. Walker very well at the time, though he calls him "a nice young fellow. . . ." He simply objected to having Hylan shelved. Only when Governor Smith campaigned against Mr. Hylan in Brooklyn in a speech which the mayor characterized as "applesauce and venom," and when the primary vote in Brooklyn returned a safe majority for Walker, did McCooey fall in line behind the "nice young fellow."

This tilt showed that John McCooey, though he might give the appearance of independent action, was not able to control, or to oppose, the organization that had put him into power. In the various offices—President of the Civil Service Commission, Deputy Collector, and Deputy Comptroller—which he held before his election as borough leader, he had always entertained a proper respect for the wishes of the party. His first political experience had taught him a good deal. Long before he got the job at Station S he used to eat lunch in a saloon run by a bullet-headed, thick-jowled gentleman who com-

manded the respect of all the bully-boys in the neighborhood. This gentleman made it a point to be on
friendly terms with everyone and often chatted
affably with McCooey while the latter was enjoying
a schooner and a sandwich. "And that," says Mc-
Cooey, "was how I met Mr. Murphy. . . ."

Like Murphy, he has come to possess in a re-
markable degree the qualities essential for boss-ship
—sensitiveness and accessibility. With the exception
of the Hylan affair, he has been on the winning, the
popular, side of most important issues. In 1911 certain critics said that he made his borough a "closed
corporation," a "Tammany Trust." There was talk
of replacing him with Augustus Van Wyck (once a
candidate for governor against Theodore Roosevelt). McCooey weathered that storm as he has
weathered the suggestion that he was in the pay of
William Randolph Hearst (an old friend), that he
had taken bribes from companies that distributed
impure food, that an unnamed "relative" had ap-
propriated $22,000 of city money, that his sister
Margaret had obtained an $8,500 school superin-
tendentship not warranted by her abilities. He stood
with Murphy for the impeachment of Governor Sul-
zer, a position dictated to him by the party; he suggested to successive Democratic conventions that
Hearst would make a good governor, and when

Hearst and Murphy fought he tried to reconcile them and did not stop trying until the Tammany leader ordered the editor's "filthy, lying newspapers" to be removed from the table in his club. In all these activities McCooey was performing very adequately a boss's function of balancing, of listening, of mollifying, of suggesting. He championed, too, issues apart from the issues championed by his party. It was not his function to champion gallant issues. It was his function to discern the winning side.

Now John McCooey, "Chairman of the Democratic Executive Committee," sits from ten-thirty to five in his office in Brooklyn. He makes no appointments. His door is never closed. Before ten o'clock a queue forms outside that open door: people from every layer of the cake—a woman who wants to get her son on the police force, an alderman, a college boy, a veteran asking the party to help him collect his pension, a top-hatted lawyer, a hod carrier—he sees them one by one. And he sounds everyone he sees on his opinions of this or that movement of the party. He is as sensitive to reactions as one of those machines that can detect an earthquake a thousand miles away. Is there talk about condemning a city area to make new streets? Nothing will be done until someone has dropped in to see McCooey. Does the Borough need more playgrounds? Will

Timmy O'Day make a good city marshal? See what
McCooey thinks. . . .

With his visitor in front of him, John McCooey
leans back in his chair, his right hand holds the lapel
of his coat, his left rests upon his stomach. Blandly
he spins out a long and apparently vapid sentence,
then smiles as if he saw his rhetoric floating in the
air. The visitor will go away, having extracted from
that floating skein just what he wanted, an accurate,
concise estimate of the party's feeling. Those houses
are too valuable to pull down; Timmy O'Day will
never do. John McCooey never refuses help and
never refuses to answer a question. He lets reporters
interrupt his shaves, his morning bath, his breakfast;
sometimes he apologizes in his youthful voice for
not talking longer. The lather, he says, is drying on
his face, or the maid is telling him that the eggs
have been on the table for ten minutes. He goes out
six nights a week to political dinners. When he is
going to spend one of his rare evenings alone he
brings home a docket of papers. He belongs to nineteen societies, including the Knights of Columbus
and the Protective Order of Elks; he is President
of the Emerald Club and of the Faithful Sons of
Saint Patrick. When he has time he plays golf. He
smokes cigars. He has a wife (considerably younger
than himself) and a married daughter; his shrewd

son, John, Jr., practises law in Brooklyn. Every year
on the sixteenth of June the party gives John Mc-
Cooey a birthday treat. Hundreds of loyal Democratic voters get on the party steamboat, the
Mandalay, and go chugging up the Hudson to Bear
Mountain, where they dine. Flying fish are not encouraged on the *Mandalay.* There is very little drinking. These voters are frugal and conservative
citizens; they bring with them their wives and pug-
nosed children. Great men make speeches; little men
eat; then all go home, sated but noisy, on the dim-
ming river.

It is hard to remember any anecdotes about John
McCooey that are worth writing down. He is too
deliberate a man to be guilty of those impromptu
turns that are the truffles of biography. Characteristic is the sentence with which, at the mayoralty
conferences, he answered every question put to him
—a sentence that is now his favorite joke. Asked
whether his golf game is any better, how he is feeling, whether he has lost any weight, he repeats his
reply: "The situation, as far as I am concerned, is
unchanged." Then there is the story of Mayor
Hylan naming a ferryboat for him . . . but rather
than this story I want to leave as colophon a picture of him that I often remember, liking it, I suppose, more for a sort of vague fitness than for any

meaning that might be read into it. I had started to call on him one evening, and as I walked along Saint Mark's Avenue in Brooklyn I knew that in another moment I would see the front of his square house. Then I did see it. Someone was there before me. The intruder still had on his hat and overcoat; he stood on the top step, outlined against the panel of the door; now he looked up at the big winter stars, and now he looked down into the street, and as I watched him it seemed to me that he was listening.

To what? There was no sound around us but the sound of the city, the multiple dim rumor of people coming and going, yet this listener was so intent that I wondered if he heard something else. He looked as if he were trying to hear a tune played by a band a long way off. My foot touched the step; the man turned. I saw that it was John McCooey.

MAN IN A BLUE SUIT

MAN IN A BLUE SUIT

THERE are professions to which people who have the faculty of not taking themselves seriously rarely belong. An undertaker with a sense of humor, for instance, would fail, perhaps disagreeably, to achieve the manner proper to his calling. Some baseball umpires have been genial fellows, but they were constrained to repress during working hours their tendency to relieve tense situations with a *bon mot* or a tolerant shrug. Bill Klem, probably the best known of contemporary umpires, is forced to make no such adjustment. Considering his work as an art, he brings to it a violent pride that eliminates the possibility of self-deprecation. Like a fighter who has never been knocked off his feet in the ring, he bases his estimate of himself on a single claim. This claim is not hidden away in his mind, and it isn't one that he emphasizes, either; to him it isn't a claim at all, but a conviction that has become as natural a part of his daily life as the sight of his face in the mirror when he is shaving. If he speaks of it at all, he does so with an arrogance far more startling than any that could be expressed by pounding the table—mentions it in passing as you might mention any fact indisputably proved and familiar to everybody. He thinks he has never made a mistake umpiring a ball game.

Bill Klem is the oldest active umpire in the major leagues. He is fifty-four. The weather has obliterated youth from his face just as it has kept away the indications of age; the thin, short hair on his bullet-like head is an indeterminate color, not gray, not brown; his skin is a bright seasoned red, and around his eyes are set permanently the lines you get for a little while if you watch something in a glare of sunlight. His nose is short and his lower lip juts out like a wind-instrument player's. He has umpired twenty-two years of professional ball and twelve World Series. In mechanical accuracy his decisions are as good as anybody's, perhaps as good as he claims, but his importance in baseball is based on more than his ability to make decisions.

A long time ago something happened that made Klem think he could handle any situation that came up. He was working in the Western Association, in a game between two bush-league towns that had carried on a long rivalry. His friends told him to look out for the captain of one of the teams, a center fielder locally famous as a fighter. It was said that this fielder played ball for the pleasure of arguing. He had beaten up several umpires. In those days the leagues had not yet adopted the present system of having one man behind the plate and another, or perhaps two more, on bases. If there was a runner on base, the single umpire stood behind the pitcher—otherwise, behind the catcher. Almost everything the umpire did was sure to be disputed; it wasn't unusual for a fellow to come in from the outfield to argue. Klem had just turned away after calling one of the visitors safe in a close play at second when he heard the crowd roar, and understood without looking that the center fielder had thrown away his glove and was running in to argue the decision.

Klem could not say afterward why he behaved the way he did. He walked to a place halfway between the pitcher's box and the plate and dug his spiked heel into the dirt and drew a line there at right angles to the patch from the plate to the pitcher's box. The crowd yelled when it saw what he meant, then kept quiet with interest. At the plate the umpire turned around for the first time. The big fielder had got to the line. For some reason he did not cross it. What would happen if he crossed the line was not defined—such gestures as the one Klem had made are formidable partly, and perhaps solely, because their meaning is vague. Klem drew a line with his heel once more, years later, in a World Series between Detroit and Chicago when players from the Chicago dugout crowded around him wrangling about the way he called the pitching. He threatened to put anyone who crossed it out of the game. Klem's line has since been made official and marked in lime in front of each dugout of a regulation field; only one player at a time from each team can cross it to argue.

Like all umpires, Klem got into his profession by accident. He grew up in Rochester in a prosperous family of German descent. His father ran a cooperage. He has five sisters, who have married citizens of Rochester and still live there; and five brothers, some of whom migrated. He played on local school and semi-professional teams and managed an amateur team of his own, but took little interest in learning a proper trade. He was timekeeper for a bridge company in Berwick, Pennsylvania, when he umpired his first game. The Berwick team had given him a percentage of the gate and a box of cigars to play first base for them on Saturday. They offered him the same pay to play again on Sunday, but he said he felt too stiff—he'd rather umpire. The manager of the town hotel told him after the game that he'd never seen a sweeter job of umpiring in his life, and Klem, who is not in the habit of regarding tributes to himself with skepticism, offered the manager one of the cigars he had earned the day before. They were silent for a moment, contemplating their smokes and spitting over the railing of the hotel porch. The manager warmed to his subject. He'd been to Philadelphia to see the big-league games and not one of the umpires they had up there had done a sweeter job, nor the whole bunch of them together. For a fellow like Klem to be timekeeper in a two-for-a-nickel bridge company when he could be earning good pay as a big-league umpire was ridiculous, the hotel keeper seemed to think. Klem agreed with him. Thousands of such conversations have taken place on the piazzas of such hotels as the Berwick House, but the odd thing about this one was that its echoes persisted. The following week, on company time, Klem studied the baseball manual, and the next Saturday told the foreman of the bridge company that he was quitting. On the following Monday he went to Philadelphia to be a big-league umpire.

Like players, most umpires begin work with a Class D team, the lowest grade of recognized professional baseball organizations, and work up through Class C, B, A, and AA teams, from shoddy country circuits to town leagues of increasing importance, until they reach a class of teams that are not indicated by a letter because they are superior to such classification—the big teams of the American and National leagues. Their progress, if they are good at their work, is rapid. Major-league clubs scout for umpires continually; the scouts are usually themselves former umpires who have got too old for active work on the diamond. Klem planned to skip his apprenticeship. Silk O'Laughlin, the foremost umpire in the American League, had gone to school with him in Rochester. In Philadelphia he watched O'Laughlin work and talked things over with him after the game. The next day he went to Bridgeport to see a former manager of the Rochester Club, who was running the team there, and the same week he umpired a game in Waterbury. Through that summer he worked in the Connecticut League, and the next year, 1903, in the New York State League. He got offers from both major leagues, joined the National at the end of the season, and before going with the eastern clubs was farmed out for a year in the Western Association.

In those days umpires who never suffered actual injury were often made sick by nervous strain. It isn't unusual even now for an umpire to go to pieces during his first seasons with a major league. Some of them lose their hair or turn gray in a year or two; others get indigestion, or contract a twitch or a skin disease. Klem suffered badly from eczema. He used to wear gray silk gloves to cover up his bandages. The players thought he was wearing them for

fashion and called him a dude. He enjoyed that. He
thought it was a bad idea to let them find out anything about him or know when he was sore, although
many of his colleagues at the time were in the habit
of backing up their opinions with punches. An umpire named Tim Herst—one of Klem's best friends
—was famous for liking a fight; if a player questioned what he said, he would step under the stands
with him right then, or go up to his hotel room after
the game and throw him under the bed and start
choking him. Herst lost his job for his informal
method of correcting Eddie Collins's manners. Collins was arguing with him when Herst suddenly
bellowed, "Git out of me way or I'll spit in your eye."
When Collins began to talk again, he let him have it.
Recognizing his own breach of decorum, he did not
fill out the report that the umpire is required to sub-
mit to the league secretary after every game. He
couldn't bear to hand in a report admitting he was
wrong.

Many of the other umpires Klem worked with
were colorful or eccentric fellows. Jim Johnson, who
patented the present official baseball mask, heard that
league officials were having him shadowed to find
out how much he drank. He stopped drinking, but
the feeling that he was the subject of investigations
never left him. One day, years after the rumored

shadowing, he and Klem were in the smoker of a
Pullman on their way West when a drummer with
an elk's tooth on his watch chain got on the train
and started talking to the two umpires in the im-
memorial manner of drummers. Klem laughed at
his stories, but Johnson wouldn't say a word; he
was nervous and kept making covert motions toward
the door. When Klem finally stepped into the aisle
with him the other umpire was trembling.

"For God's sake, don't talk to that guy in there."

"Why not?"

"Maybe you're so dumb you can't see," Johnson
whispered furiously. "But, anyway, I'm telling you
—he's a detective."

One of the changes in umpiring that have come
about in the twenty-five years since Klem joined the
National League is the present system of emphasiz-
ing decisions. An umpire never used to let the crowd
hear what he said. You had to tell from the
action of the players whether he had called a runner
safe or out or a pitched ball good. Once, in Chicago,
where Klem was disliked, a player of the Chicago
team hit a long ball along the right-field foul line in
the eighth inning with a man on base. Klem called
the ball foul, but the batter, paying no attention,
rounded first and went on to second, and his team
mate, who had been on first, ran home. If the run

had been allowed it would have tied the score, and when Klem insisted the ball was foul and sent the batter back to the plate and the scoring player back to base, the crowd came down on the field to get him. He escaped by running back to the dressing room. He made up his mind that the crowd should have heard his decision at the time the hit was made. At present he makes himself clear on all occasions. When he is behind the catch and a strike is pitched, his right arm moves up with an imperative motion and his roared word can be heard all over the field. No other umpire calls them as loud as Klem. On bases, where he has more room to move in, he is even more theatrical. To sight a hit close to the foul line, he runs to the line and jumps as he gets to it, coming down as the ball comes down. Calling a runner out, he points to the bench with an impetus that seems enough by itself to sweep the fellow in the direction indicated; if the man on base is safe after a close play, Klem leans forward, violently bringing both hands forward with their palms toward the ground and making them vibrate as though to indicate that they had taken that position at the dictation of some omniscient and infallible force of which he is merely the interpreter.

During the wintertime most umpires get civil jobs. One of them used to be a floorwalker in Franklin

Simon's. Others are clerks, farmers, coaches of
school basketball or football teams. Klem has never
done anything while the clubs are resting. He says
he is an umpire, and that's enough. He is married
and lives in a modest house in Miami. His salary has
risen by prescribed steps from the twenty-five
hundred dollars of a young umpire in his first season
to the twelve thousand dollars that are top wages in
his profession. A few years ago some land he owned
in Florida got to be worth a quarter of a million
dollars on paper, and the rumor went around that
Klem was going to sell out and retire. He held on too
long and his paper profits grew less and at last
dwindled away altogether. He took his loss
philosophically.

During the season he officiates at an average of six
games a week. He plays golf in his spare time. One
winter day somebody saw him on the beach at Miami,
performing curious evolutions. He bent forward
with his hands on his knees, then straightened up,
jerking his arms. He swung round on his heel, pointing to various parts of the horizon while his lips
moved silently but emphatically. He crouched forward with his palms toward the sand. He was
shadow-umpiring.

Umpires are a solitary clan. They don't go on
parties with players whose games they arbitrate,

or eat with them, or train with them. When a club is
on tour, they travel apart from the team—in another
car and, when possible, in another train. Klem knows
every ball player you can think of; none of them is
his friend. Most of them admire his work, but don't
know what he is like off the field. His only intimates
are other umpires, a few officials like President
Heydler of the National League, and the older generation of baseball writers. The managers of the
hotels he uses traveling around the circuit have
known him for years, and many of them make a point
of having dinner with him whenever he is in their
town. His mind apparently keeps a photographic
record of every play he has seen, and as he talks,
particularly if he is touching on his own exploits, he
dramatizes everything, waving his arms; his voice
gets high and hoarse and his red face redder.

"Don't get excited, Bill," his wife says if she is
around.

"By God!" Klem answers with hoarse intensity.
"Am I excited? I've never been calmer in my life."

Off the field he wears, at all times of the year,
neat blue clothes not unlike an umpire's uniform,
except that they lack the pocket for balls that runs
across the short tails of the official suit. In action, he
keeps five or six balls in this pocket, working them
round behind him so they won't be against his side to

bruise him if he is knocked down. His stocky figure seems bigger when he is umpiring; he is important then, dominating twin forces—the crowd whose suspense pushes down behind him, and the players moving in front of him in changing, concentrated patterns. He is sincere in his belief that he has never made a mistake on the field. His pride, the quality that makes him unusual, is rooted in that belief. If he ever suspected himself of being fallible he would begin to worry and brood about his decisions. If he ever called a ball wrong and recognized it afterward, I honestly believe he'd quit the game.

OVER BABEL

OVER BABEL

H EIGHT, six feet two inches . . . weight one hundred eighty-two pounds . . . measurement of skull twenty-three and three-quarters inches . . . a dreamer . . ."

Thus a phrenologist, bringing scales and tape measure to the support of a science now somewhat outmoded, charted the body and soul of Irving T. Bush.

Even had he added that Mr. Bush's nose turns up at the end, that his mouth turns down at the corners, that his eyes are brown and his fingers spatulate, the phrenologist would not have summarized Mr. Bush completely. No summary of Mr. Bush is complete that does not make clear that this is the man who has his office in the conspicuous top floor of the Bush Building, that Gothic tower, many-windowed, brilliantly lighted at night, over the Babel of Forty-second Street. And this is the man who conceived and built the vast organization known as the Bush Terminal, which spreads in docks and warehouses and railroad tracks over two hundred and fifty acres of Brooklyn waterfront.

The Bush Terminal remains the most important

thing about Irving T. Bush. To get this achievement down on paper one has to go back to the beginning, even at the risk of stating facts that everybody knows.

Twenty years ago, before this terminal had set a
model for other terminals of the same kind, the
streets of New York were filled with big horses pulling loads of freight. A great many cargoes came
in on boats or freight trains and had to be hauled
through the streets to warehouses or to other docks
or freight stations for reshipment. Each transfer in-
volved large expense. Armadas of truck wagons tied
up the downtown traffic. Irving Bush saw a way to
combine docks, warehouses, and freight lines in a
single plant. Ships berthed at the docks of this organization could unload directly into warehouses or
into freight cars, and vice versa.

All his life Irving Bush had been thinking about
the harbor. His father was president of an oil refinery in Brooklyn. The family grew up in one of
those old houses on Columbia Heights, the lawns of
which, equipped with nymphs and metal animals, plunged steeply toward the river. On Sundays
young Irving listened to the sermons of Henry
Ward Beecher. On weekdays he watched the ships
go up and down. He went to the Hill School in
Pottstown, Pa. When college was suggested, he said

he would rather work in the Bush oil refinery. Before he took up his duties his father gave him a trip around the world in a sailing yacht, the *Coronet*. He was cruising somewhere in the Red Sea when the idea for the terminal occurred to him. Soon after his return his father died. The Standard Oil Company bought the family refinery and for a while Irving Bush worked for the Standard Oil Company, but the idea of the terminal stuck in his mind and his plans ripened. In 1901 he bought a second-hand towboat, some second-hand rails, and a second-hand locomotive. He bought a warehouse and built a dock. He called his establishment the Bush Terminal.

For a long time it did not pay. There is an amusing story about the bales of hay with which Irving Bush started operations: to show the railroads that there was a Bush Terminal, he had a man send him the hay, twenty-five carloads of it, from Michigan, giving freight contracts only with the specification that the hay be delivered on the tracks of the Bush Terminal—and when the hay was delivered, he simulated a great rush of business by having it shunted around on his rusty, second-hand tracks and loaded and unloaded in and out of empty warehouses by employees who loudly hinted that their overlord was suffering from a cerebral derangement. But now the railroads knew about the Bush Terminal, and

slowly manufacturers and shipping companies came
to know about it. Irving Bush's prosperity increased,
and with the prosperity came the thunder of great
facts about the terminal. It expanded to include a
hundred and twenty-three warehouses and eight
piers. Now Mr. Bush pays taxes of a thousand dollars a day, and his profits have reached about a million and a half a year.

Going down the river on his yearly trips to
Europe he can look at the enterprise which he has
built and which has helped to bring order into the
chaos of the harbor. Palled in mist, on its gray
acres, the terminal stretches, big and dim; warehouses bulk behind the low oblongs of the docks;
freight tracks run up and down in all directions and
in the distance, over the masts, the smokestacks, the
nervous arms of cranes, hangs the curve of Brooklyn
Bridge, a paper shadow in the sky. It must be a sat-
isfactory sight for him. Under this expansive pattern, the terminal functions tirelessly as a sort of
clearing house. Its profits are derived from dock
rental, storage charges, and from commissions for
shipping freight. The beginning of the enterprise
was made possible by money that Mr. Bush inherited
from his father, but in so far as Mr. Bush planned
this terminal, and built it, little by little, as he had
planned it, it is very much his own.

While Irving Bush was working out his plan for the terminal, the family that had lived among the metal animals in the big house over the river had broken up. His brother, Wendall T. Bush, went to Columbia, wrote some verses, and when he graduated, persuaded his father to buy him a magazine. Mr. Bush, senior, being of a pious turn of mind, bought the *Brooklyn Churchman* from Edward Bok. "But I want to change the name," Wendall Bush told Mr. Bok, "not just Brooklyn, you know—this magazine is going to be something wider, something that will be read all over the world. . . ." Mr. Bok suggested that he call it the *Cosmopolitan,* and under this title and another owner (for Wendall Bush failed to make a go of it) the *Cosmopolitan* achieved a prestige slightly different but fully as formidable as that which it had enjoyed under the stencil of the Church. Irving Bush, meanwhile, went to Lakewood, where he played polo, entertained a good deal, and took the club car up to town every weekday morning.

In 1917 when the United States entered the war the government gave Irving Bush three sonorous titles—Chief of Embarkation, Director of Harbor and Terminal Facilities, and Chief Executive Official of the War Board of the Port of New York. He became very busy.

After the armistice he went abroad to study conditions, saw Trotsky and Stinnes, and gave his opinions on these gentry in cautious interviews with steamship reporters. "Studying conditions" is one of his favorite pastimes; it amounts with him to a prolonged and perhaps subconscious consideration of symptoms and statistics terminating suddenly in a decision which may be extremely obvious or extremely far-fetched, but which is pretty generally accurate. As a corollary to this system of intuitive economics there seems to be in Irving Bush a wish to project himself into the future. Friends wondered why he built that Bush Tower on Forty-second Street since he was only going to use three rooms in it. One editorial writer suggested that Mr. Bush, a Pharaoh of Finance, was putting up this office building as kings put up tombs, because he wanted to be remembered. This theory was correct. When Mr. Bush built the Bush House in London, an immense office building on the Strand, he set in the foundations a lead box full of documents intended to inform the people who open it in two thousand years about our civilization. When he asked H. G. Wells what to put in the box, the world's historian suggested a bottle of pickles, a safety razor, a cotton reel, a book on how to behave, a sewing machine, a dressing kit, a movie reel, Whitaker's Almanac, and Bradshaw's Continental time-table.

Now sixty-one years old, Irving Bush still drives himself along with the uneven, angry energy of a man who has been confronted all his life with the opportunity to loaf. On sunny mornings he gets up at six forty-five. He walks from his apartment to the Riding Club and orders his horse; then he goes to Childs Restaurant on Fifty-ninth Street and eats breakfast. By the time he has finished his oatmeal and tea his horse is saddled. He rides for half an hour in the Park, then goes back to his apartment and changes his clothes for business.

Mr. Bush served two terms as president of the New York State Chamber of Commerce and was popular, although at times he tried to make the Chamber support causes in which it felt little interest. Like so many men of impulsive temperament, he is apt to be victimized by his enthusiasms.

For instance, although, unlike most industrial men, he does not pretend to be a connoisseur in matters of art, he was greatly taken with a picture painted by George Inness, the seventy-year-old son of the great landscape artist, showing Jesus Christ looking down a sunbeam at a city wasted by war. The picture was entitled "The Only Hope." Mr. Bush asked the Chamber to arrange for the exhibition of this picture as an object lesson in all the big cities in the country and was exceedingly annoyed when certain Chambermen of Jewish faith, unable to share the conviction suggested by the title, vetoed the proposal.

Irving Bush makes up for being, in artistic matters, one of the people who know what they like by being, in religious matters, one of the people who believe what they like. He is a Congregationalist because his father was a Congregationalist, but he does not altogether accept the Congregational Church or reject any other. "I believe," he says, "that a man can worship God as well in a Moslem temple as in a Gothic nave, and as well in his office as in either."

As to the particular form of worship that goes on in the churchly and many-windowed tower that Mr. Bush has built over Forty-second Street, this apothegm supplies no clue. When he is in New York he spends six or seven hours a day in his tower. His office is not very big, since, being at the top of the tower, space is limited. You go up to the twenty-sixth floor in an express elevator and take a private elevator to the twenty-ninth. In an outer room sits a stenographer and an elderly man named Jones, who has been Mr. Bush's secretary for thirty years. Inside, on Mr. Bush's desk, are two telephones, a bottle of mineral water, some papers, a can of cigarettes, and a package of salted almonds; the walls are covered with framed photographs of Mr. Bush, of his buildings, of his son, of his yachts, of his villas, of his father. Under each window flows a gray river, and the two rivers are suave and docile as if they were maritime etchings hung there to give an appropriate atmosphere. Little boats move on them, and even gulls are visible, twirling like pieces of foil in the sunlight over the gray water.

Irving Bush long ago stopped bothering about details of work at the terminal; he merely passes on questions of policy, on appropriations, on changes. The hours he spends in his office are chiefly taken up with personal affairs, with letters to men who ask his advice on business projects, and with projects like that of the Inness picture, which for the moment are enjoying his interest. He writes a good deal—business articles for *System* and editorials in *Fore and Aft,* a sheet issued to the employees of the Bush Terminal. If a magazine editor wants a business article he can always get it by telephoning Irving Bush.

Like all magnates who, growing older, have turned their attention to generalities, his life has lost some of the urgency that made it once significant and picturesque. But if a certain importance has slipped away from the things he does now, that importance was buried long ago in the mechanism of the terminal by the river. A hundred and sixty thousand freight cars were loaded at the terminal last year. Ships from five continents and twenty-five nations tie up there. There are twenty-six million cubic feet of warehouse space at the terminal. Its docks are the biggest in the world. . . . Such facts make you less interested in what Mr. Bush is than in what he has done until you remember that between being and doing, no line has ever been drawn; if the facts about the terminal belong anywhere they belong here— place-marks, chapter headings, in an American biography.

SNOW MAN

SNOW MAN

BEFORE I met Urbain Ledoux, or even knew who he was, I saw him in a subway train. The car was almost empty (it was after four in the morning) and he was sitting with his eyes closed, a big man with a handsome and pictorial face that made him look a little like an actor, although his clothes were not at all the clothes an actor would have thought of, being simply a strong cover for his body: corduroy suit, thick rubbers, a soft hat, a leather jacket. At Eighth Street he got out of the train. He was carrying a parcel. Three years later I found out his name.

For a long time he had no name at all. When the men among whom he worked asked what to call him he said, "Nothing," and an Associated Press correspondent turned this into "Mr. Zero." Once, at a meeting, he said that his name was Urbain, and the next day an editorial writer discoursed on "The Work of Brother Urbain" as if he were a sort of black friar. Other writers have made him out a philanthropic buffoon, a crazy saint of beaten people. All these labels of what he is are meaningless against the fact that last year he fed 250,000 hungry men.

He fed most of them in a place called "The Tub," a canteen that he ran in the cellar under an old house in St. Mark's Place. The rent of this place was thirty dollars a month. The arrangements were simple: bare table, wooden chairs, white walls, a lithograph of the steamship *Majestic,* a victrola, a bin for old clothes, another for food, a canteen booth by the door where each man coming in gave a meal ticket or a five-cent piece in exchange for a tin coffee cup, a tin bowl for soup, a spoon. Rye bread was piled in dishes on each table. The men took the thick slices and mashed them in the soup. They could have their bowls filled as often as they liked. They did not spill anything. They ate intensely and without haste. They did not look at each other.

The nickel paid for what each man ate. The Tub was not a charity, nor is the haven that has taken its place; nor does Urbain Ledoux, in theory, give anything but his services. He buys food in quantity at very low prices: frozen potatoes, last year's beans, macaroni sweepings, yesterday's loaves of Jewish bread, recovered fats, preserves in cans whose labels have been spoiled by fire or in transportation. He occasionally takes contributions when they are offered. He does not ask for them.

His friends send him old clothes. He boils the starch out of dress shirts and gives them away. "Damned uncomfortable things," he says. "I used to wear them myself. . . ."

He was not born to formal linen. His father, Joseph Ledoux, was a laborer and later a bookseller in Connecticut; after some prosperous years he went to Canada and bought a farm. Urbain Ledoux was born at St. Hélène, in the Province of Quebec, in 1878. He went to school at Sainte Marie de Manoir and worked his way through a Catholic seminary at Van Buren, Maine. After graduation he worked as overseer in cotton mills at Biddeford, Maine, and wrote for the Montreal *Figaro*. A man he disliked was asking for the American consulship at Three Rivers; he competed, got the appointment, served as consul successively at Bordeaux and in Santos, Brazil. He was given the consulship at Prague and there enjoyed grand days; he belonged to the Nobility Club where—the only member without a title—he played baccarat with visiting Hohenzollerns. At the age of thirty-two he resigned from the consular service and came to New York; friends he had made at Prague offered him new opportunities. He promoted sales campaigns, organized, among other things, a company for making industrial alcohol, and lived very well at the Park Avenue

Hotel. Up to this time the most important factor in his career had been his energy. At first he was energetic rather than ambitious, but as he reached higher and everything he wanted fell to him, he began for the first time to question the glory of having played cards at the Nobility Club. Aware of a flaw in his content, he started a long discussion with himself, based on a heterogeneous reading of Russian mystics and French novelists, and illustrated with texts from the Greek: "Know Thyself." "To serve—the highest good."

At first the thing that he picked out to serve was not clearly defined. During the war he served the Labor Bureau. Then he threw himself into the work of organizing meetings in Boston for the World Peace Foundation. It was still not what he wanted. The idea of serving mankind, a shrouded figure, came slowly to be replaced by the figures of the jobless men he saw in Boston. One day he asked such a man to take off his shirt. He stood the man on the bandstand in Boston Common.

It was near noontime. A good many jobless men were sitting on the benches in the Common. Some clerks, too, were smoking there while they digested the sandwiches and sundaes they had eaten for lunch. A crowd collected, and Urbain Ledoux began to auction the man who had taken off his shirt.

Big and burly, with his face of an actor or a general, he stormed beside the partly naked man on the bandstand, pointing to the thin ribs that stuck through his flesh like the ribs of a bird. "See, he is thin," he said. "He wants to work. Give him some work and he'll get fat again." In this way he found jobs for a few men, but before long he was banished from the Common. It was an unseemly thing, even a reflection against the city, many persons thought, to use the Common for any such purpose. Urbain Ledoux came back to New York and went to live on the Bowery. He found dirty, ragged, and sick men sleeping in doorways and on the floors of vacant buildings. He tried to get food for them, working at first with the Salvation Army and then, in 1921, starting his own canteen, which he called, "The Old Bucks and Lame Ducks Club."

Only old men who were sick or crippled could eat at the Old Bucks and Lame Ducks Club. Urbain Ledoux could feed only a few and he turned away all who were not both old and sick, but in 1922, when the city was filled with unemployed, he decided that a man who could not get a job was in actuality a cripple —old, too, since he was without hope. He fed everyone who came. On New Year's Day he marched a squad of tatterdemalions to the White House and had them join the line of guests who were being received by President Harding. The President shook hands with them. Mr. Zero's name was in the headlines, but things were going badly with the old bucks and lame ducks. Since he had no money himself, he asked each man to pay two cents, thinking that would cover the cost of the meal. He had reckoned normal appetites. The intense, steady eating of the starved men made a deficit, and he raised the price to five cents and reorganized the club.

It was then that he named it "The Tub"—a reference, vague and grandiose, to Diogenes. His idealism also is vague and grandiose, the kind of idealism that could inspire action only in a man who responds with action to every stimulus. He put a motto on the wall telling the purpose of The Tub: "To bring a greater share of love and beauty into the lives of those too long deprived." That his idea of love and beauty should be rye bread and bean soup is what makes this man extraordinary and makes him noble. He is an idealist, if one may define that term as meaning a person who passes from a remote concept to an immediate deed without the middle stage of criticism. He is not particularly kind-hearted. Particularly kind-hearted people are seldom much good at helping the poor—they give what they have to the first affliction they see. Urbain Ledoux judges shrewdly between degrees of desperation. A man asks him for an overcoat. He will not get it. The coat will go to another—weaker, older, or just dismissed from a hospital. He sifts panhandlers from the true derelicts who look just like them. But all this is giving an unfair idea of him, for although his pity is diffused, he has never been able to harden himself against suffering. There are old men whom he keeps all winter; and when the spring comes he cannot turn them out. He feeds them until June is in the parks, warming the benches on which they will sit, and it is time for him to go away.

In the summers he earns the money that pays his personal expenses for the rest of the year. Sometimes he organizes a sales campaign for a manufacturing company. Last year he bought second-hand books in New York and sold them to libraries in Montreal. All winter, out of his profits he donates five-cent pieces to men who come into his haven without any money at all. These are the saddest of all scavengers; they have failed so often that they do not dare ask even for five cents on the street. A man who is sick can eat in the haven as often as he likes. An old man can eat there as often as he likes. The rest can eat once. No repeaters. "Pull your chairs in close, boys," shouts Mr. Zero. "When you've eaten, get out. . . . For God's sake put the coffeepot on the table; don't keep running up and down with your cups."

When Henry Ford sailed to end the war in
Europe, Mr. Zero had three tickets for the trip. He
arrived at the dock late. The peace ship, surrounded
by cartoonists, was already in the middle of the East
River. Without a moment's hesitation Mr. Zero
plunged into the water, festooned with lovely ara-
besques of oil, and began swimming after the ship.
The wharfmen who rescued him refused to put him
on board. "There's enough nuts there already," they
said. . . .

Once he was arrested in Washington. Carrying
a lighted lantern, he picketed the building where the
disarmament conferences were being held. What, he
asked the police, could they do to him for carrying a
lantern? "I was looking for a Christian among the
delegates." He defined Christian as "one who practises the gentility of Christ." He holds preachermen
in a certain suspicion. Before the spokesman of any
organized church can talk to Mr. Zero's guests he
has to put up a hundred dollars to go in the soup—
and then he may not talk for more than half an hour.

Urbain Ledoux used to live in a back room littered with books, at 16 St. Mark's Place, where he
cooked his own meals. Except to work, he goes out
very little. Although he has never elected the lot of
an anchorite, most of the bonds that tie men to a conventional routine are, for him, broken; his first wife

is dead, his daughter married, his son, a boy of
seventeen, whom he supports, goes to boarding
school in the winter and works in the summer. Last
summer he married an actress named Mary Lewis.
He says she will help him carry on his work.

Up to this time the loneliness, like the isolation of
the men he feeds, that had descended round him,
tended to accentuate in him that complacency evident
in all people who have sacrificed something to an
ideal. He talked about himself, impersonally and at
length, in the admiring terms of one who has been
much impressed with a biography which he has read
too hastily to grasp all its details. But this uncertain
conception of himself, the constant need to under-
score the purposes which, like chapter headings, inform his daily life, have had no counterpart in his
competence to do practical work.

He gets up at three in the morning. At five he
puts on his leather coat and goes to the All Night
Mission, the Hadley Street Mission, and other charity headquarters where he gives meal tickets ("Good
for All You Can Eat at Mr. Zero's") to the men
who have been sleeping there. Meals are served at
twelve and five. On rainy days the place opens fifteen
minutes before the hour. When they have eaten, the
raggedest of the men come and ask him for clothes.
He has few to give away. Bundles come in from

friends, from casual people who have heard him speak and wanted to help him. He has never received any important gifts of money. Once a Senator gave him five hundred dollars to help the men who, in 1922, had no jobs.

That was the biggest gift Mr. Zero ever accepted; ordinarily he rejects such offers—the work is not a charity, he insists—but under special conditions he admits exceptions to his rule of self-reliance. And when conditions are worse than usual, when it snows, and many have no work, he runs a special bread line on the Bowery. The men, a thousand at a time, stand close to the curb, bent over to keep their collars against their necks. With snow on his cap and his shoulders and arms, and clinging in scales to his coat and to the stern cornices of his eyebrows, Mr. Zero, with the gestures of an orator, the voice of a ringmaster, and the shining red face of a police-man being decorated for bravery, directs the giving out of coffee and bread.

THE IMMIGRANT

THE IMMIGRANT

STORIES about Benjamin Winter began to go round when he made his first big turns in real estate, some five or six years ago. It was natural for people to talk about him because nobody knew him; then, too, his career lent itself well to fable.

Soon the stories bloomed with amazing variations. What had been stereotyped success-spreads in the *Cosmopolitan Magazine* suddenly began to climb and blossom; and when he bought the W. K. Vanderbilt house, the Vincent Astor house, and the old Jay Gould riding academy, rumor erupted, like a magician's rosebush, with flowery sprays of legend. People said that Benjamin Winter, a peasant, had sworn to avenge himself on aristocracy for the wrongs he had suffered under its heel in Poland. Then there was a preposterous tale to the effect that he was a realtor against his will—that he had a genius for painting. The newspaper men who went to interview him after one of his transactions tried to find out what had set these stories going.

They found a short Jew in a prismatic tie talking cryptically into the telephone. His face—rather

Napoleonic, slightly blue about the jaw—his semi-soft collar, and the body whose energetic fleshiness surged beneath a pin-stripe cheviot were not in any respect arresting; in fact, they quite obviously had their counterparts in the faces and bodies and clothes of innumerable business men of his age and race. When he began to talk he evidently had at the tip of his tongue some ripe formulas to use on press men. "Yes, my days I keep busy with business and my nights with communal affairs. Social gatherings and like that, charities, good fellowship. I am tired after talking all day in big figures trying so everybody will get a fair proposition. So then I go to my home, 276 Riverside Drive, ten rooms, and wash and slip on my tuxeeda and go and attend my communal affairs. . . ." He stopped, noticing with annoyance that the poised pencils were idle. It was the familiar clap-trap—the cinema of the bigwig posturing before an unreal desk until it is time for him to preside at the collations of phantom boosters.

The reporters went away irritated. Somewhere, under this blurred generalization, was a personality. What he had done proved that, in spite of the brittle attitude which for some reason he wanted people to mistake for his mind, in spite of the queer, bodiless stories that glittered like fox fire around his reputation. Whether these stories amused Benjamin Zimar of Poland has never been discovered.

That is a name that has been ascribed to him. At least, it is the name for winter in Polish, and publicity juntos of a romantic turn gave it to him in the conviction that no newspaper reader would believe that a successful Jew had retained his baptismal label. As a matter of fact the name to which he was born, in 1886, in Lodz, was Winter. His family was of a remote German descent and his father, Michael, made an excellent living marketing to retailers the products of the factories of Lodz— towels, gloves, millinery, shoes, umbrellas, mechanical pianos. And the one touch of fantasy in the life of Michael Winter is that he wanted his son to paint portraits. In his own youth he had gone to school with a boy whose talent had taken him to an atelier and then to Warsaw where he painted the wives of noblemen. Michael, the jobber, never saw him again, but whenever he found the painter's name in a newspaper he cut out the item and spoke proudly of his friendship with this man who had forgotten him. When young Benjamin displayed a knack for reproducing household shapes in crayon —"Cat," "Plate," "Mama"—Michael, the jobber, sent him away to learn painting.

He did not stay long in art school. There was

sickness in Lodz; hard times arrived, and with them, one day, a neighbor who had made money in America. He told Michael Winter how things were across the water. That winter the jobber talked excitedly to his wife, and in the spring, when the glittering neighbor went back, Michael went with him. In a few years he sent passage money for the woman and younger children. Benjamin, then twenty, worked his way to a ship at Rotterdam; his father met him one windy Monday at Ellis Island. That evening Benjamin Winter studied the want ads and borrowed a pair of overalls. On Tuesday he applied for work as a house painter.

All self-made men do these things. It would be gratifying to note that the following week he began to squander his wages and keep bad company. One finds, however, that he made no effort to mend the plot of the Great American Fairy Story. Instead, he got his rent free by painting his landlord's tenements. In 1912 he went into real estate, taking over some tenements that were not renting well, and in 1913 he formed a partnership with an Irishman. Ten years from the day that partnership was sealed, his career had progressed to its best chapter—the one in which he passed Ellis Island bound the other way, romping home to Lodz on his first holiday, a millionaire.

Straddling a chair in the finest hotel in Lodz he filled in, for a marveling audience, the gaps in his story. He had had trouble that first Tuesday; his father knew little English and he knew none, but they got a man in a Polish delicatessen to read the want ads to them. By the time he left the man who gave him his first work and started in for himself as a painting contractor, he had saved a little money; and all his savings and a good deal of luck were behind that first tottering venture in tenement-house real estate. Then Andrew O'Brien came along, a shrewd Scotch-Irishman without eyebrows or affectations and with a perpetual air of having just been interrupted in the middle of a witticism. They rented an office at One Hundred and Fiftieth Street and Broadway.

It was a successful combination. O'Brien had a photographic mind that retained every clause of an intricate lease, every scrawl on the post-no-bill-board of a proffered site; Winter's thoughts motioned on like clouds, piling and dissolving in tiers and terraces as the citadels of dream rose and fell. O'Brien could interest a client, but Winter could get a bank to extend a note that should have been called in a month before. His instinct for property drove him to curious decisions, snap judgments, apparently made on the instant; several times he bought in three minutes some site that more experienced operators had rejected after weeks of deliberation. But his instinct was never wrong. He and O'Brien moved out of their first office and began to trade in lots on Washington Heights. Then they bought their first apartment house.

Something of the magic of their rise after that must have lit his talk in the Grand Hotel. And how were things in Lodz? There had been more typhus, a neighbor told him; the poor were dying, without medicines, without bread. Benjamin Winter sent the local relief committee a check for $50,000 in American money, and at the fêtes which followed he told how he had made that money three days before he left New York by buying and selling the Claridge Hotel.

The gift was a generous one, for his profits at that time were purely paper. Much of Winter's profits are still paper, a condition common to all big plungers, but whatever proportions his wealth actually assumes, the most conservative estimate of the property he at present controls fixes the value at $40,000,000.

When he returned to his Park Avenue office, fixed resplendently forever in the hearts of the people of Lodz, it was noticed that a new dignity had come to him. It was then that he began to work at that series of operations that have made him famous across the continent.

First came the Jay Gould house in West Fifty-eighth Street. Then he bought the line of baroque atrocities that used to abut on Seventh Avenue at Fifty-eighth Street: brownstone and marble apartment houses with plush carpets and elevators that a Negro boy operates with a cable, collectively known as "Spanish Flats." The price was $7,000,000. The Vincent Astor house cost him $3,500,000 and he picked up, for $4,000,000, the W. K. Vanderbilt house, the price including the inlaid ormolu bathtub in which Mrs. Vanderbilt used to wash in the days when she was trying to find four hundred nice people in New York. After the sale a sort of farewell party was held downstairs for the benefit of one of Mr. Winter's charities. Ted Lewis played in a half-dismantled salon, and people got into the dining room for a dollar who couldn't have set foot there for any sum when the guests of the late dowager consumed birds and wine under the soundless glass Niagara of the chandelier. Later the house was thrown open to the public for one week, for an admission fee of fifty cents. The sightseers stared at the faded elegance and told each other in whispers how this man Winter had sworn to get even with aristocracy.

As a matter of fact, he is quite devoid of social consciousness. To realize this one has only to behold him, with a paper cap on his head, making loud mirth at the banquets he gives for the janitors of his numerous apartment houses. Perhaps he is subtly aware that his power depends on that Olympian vulgarity that shaped him in its mold long ago, blew luck into his mouth, and pushed him, a stubborn bubble, up to glory. At any rate, he has resolutely refused to adopt any of the pretensions that money makes so easy. He has never pretended, on Long Island, to be a country squire, nor does he own a bungalow in Maine; he likes to declare with a great guffaw that his only rural excursions are those which take him every Sunday to visit his mother in Hoboken. He sends his three small children to Public School 93, and he permits his chauffeur, a lank Swede named Henry Anderson, to treat him as an equal. At prize fights and bicycle races Mr. Winter and Henry Anderson and Mrs. Winter generally occupy adjoining seats; sometimes an acquaintance sits with them. One evening such an acquaintance, who had several times enjoyed Henry Anderson's company at a public function, ventured to protest; he pointed out that though Henry Anderson was charming, he did not belong to society.

"Listen," Winter said, "a feller can drive a car

without he is a momzer. . . . Look next time and you'll see him sitting like my pal alongside me and my wife the same way. . . ."

The people whose houses he has bought for office sites were not quite so tolerant, and they spoke another language, but if one stops to ask which clan more accurately represents the city, the answer is obvious. Benjamin Winter has counterparts wherever you turn; men who share his crudities and loyalties, who speak and dress as he does. In a way he sums up these scurrying simulacra; he has made himself, in some measure, inclusive. If the power he finds in himself has made him look like all the rest, let it go; if his collar is too tight, if his larynx is in his nose, if his grammar comes unbuttoned, forget it. He is an important New Yorker.

FRONT, BOY

FRONT, BOY

LUCIUS BOOMER wears a pince-nez, stiff cuffs, and a solitaire pearl; he is tall, shrewd, affable, good-looking and precise; he has a short nose and a high forehead; he talks with exceptional eloquence and clarity. He smokes cigars, plays golf, goes abroad every summer, and is a millionaire. Nothing about him suggests his real story. Lucius Boomer is president of the company that operates the Sherry-Netherland, the Waldorf Astoria, Sherry's, and owns the Bellevue-Stratford in Philadelphia, the Willard in Washington, the Windsor in Montreal, and the Savarin restaurants. He began his career rolling barrels in the storeroom of a resort house in Manhattan Beach.

In telling a story of this kind the rule is to begin with some dramatic moment; I think first of the night two years ago when the scaffolding around the tower of the Sherry-Netherland Hotel caught fire. Lucius Boomer stood in the crowd for three or four hours looking up. I know an associate who was called to his side at that time. I tried to make him tell me how Mr. Boomer had behaved, what he had said,

237

but he couldn't think of anything. "He was pretty quiet, he just said what he had to."

A man watching a skyscraper in which he held important interests blaze like a wax match in the soft spring evening contained only a small part of the real qualities of the affair. To understand his attitude that evening you have to know more about Lucius Boomer.

His family were hard-working people and, like many Americans of pioneer stock, inconvenienced by having to make money. When he was born his father was a young engineer living in Poughkeepsie and helping to build the railroad bridge. After the bridge was finished Mr. Boomer senior went to Chicago to work on another construction job. He died there when Lucius Boomer was eighteen. In a room in a Chicago boarding house the son of the dead engineer sat down to review his situation and decide how he was going to get along.

For a year before his father's death Lucius Boomer had been a student in the University of Chicago. He had only one facility that would help him make a living—he knew how to play the violin. His family had had him taught because they thought it would be nice for him to play some instrument; he had done unexpectedly well at it; he had played in private musicales and a few professional

concerts organized by his teachers. A week after
his father died he stopped to see an old German
violin maker who had given him his first lesson.
The old man asked him what he was going to do;
when he heard that young Boomer had only enough
money left to pay his board and room for two
months, he offered to lend him money to go to Germany and study the violin. The teacher's belief that
he could become a great violinist moved and excited
the boy, but it did not convince him. The risk was
too great; if he did not, after all, become a concert
artist there was no living in it; he might be fiddling
in a movie house some day. Instead of going to
Germany he studied stenography and got a job with
the Chicago, Milwaukee & St. Paul Railroad for
fifty dollars a month.

His next chance to make a decision came when he
got a letter from his father's former secretary, a
man who was working as clerk in one of the hotels
of the Flagler System in Florida. "I'm getting out
of here," he wrote to Lucius Boomer; "if you hustle
down you might get my job." Boomer read the letter
as he walked along State Street. An uneven, chilly
wind was driving in from the lake. Soon it would
be winter; he was not able to buy an overcoat; he
hadn't been able to save anything out of his fifty
a month. Well, he thought, in Florida he wouldn't

need a coat. He asked the general passenger agent of the Chicago-Milwaukee to give him a pass South.

The hotel job was still open, but Lucius Boomer didn't fill it. There was an epidemic of typhoid in Florida that year; three weeks after his arrival he caught typhoid and went to the hospital until spring. That was bad luck. There were lots of other men with typhoid in the hospital. One of them was a man named Joseph P. Greaves; he owned a hotel. That was good luck. Joseph Greaves owned a hotel at Manhattan Beach. He gave Boomer a job in his cellar storeroom. That was the cellar in which his rise really began.

Manhattan Beach was a smart resort in those days. There were fireworks and bicycle races and in the cool of the evening Sousa's band played on the esplanade. Lucius Boomer rolled barrels in the cellar of the Oriental Hotel. The work agreed with him; he got back some of the strength he had lost when he was sick. When fall came he went back to Florida as a bookkeeper. He had a new ambition, and he thought if he was a bookkeeper he would have time to read. He wanted to be a lawyer. Until his eyes went bad he wrote figures all day and read law books half the night. He decided that although he had gone into the hotel business only to keep warm he would have to stay in it to keep from going

blind. He had less chance of becoming a lawyer than
he had had, a few years earlier, of becoming a
violinist. He came to New York and hung around
the Hotel Plaza until he got a job as secretary to
Mr. Frederick Sterry, the manager.

Years later, when he had become a rich man,
Lucius Boomer wrote a book about his business,
Hotel Management, published by Harpers', a clearly
written, elaborately appendixed volume which is a
standard work on hotels. To read the thirty-five
main chapter heads will convince any one that a
modern hotel is as intricate as a city and as closely
coördinated as a gasoline motor. Boomer probably
learned from Sterry some of the secrets of hotel
efficiency, the devices that must be used in bringing
together in a single plant everything necessary to
make the lives of many residents with varying tastes
move with a maximum of satisfaction. He adopted
novel suggestions. He has his staff study the taste
of each guest. If a guest, in one visit, comments
favorably on the pattern of the rug, the curtain, the
bedspread, the same pattern will be on his floor or
window or bed when he comes next time. In the
McAlpin he started the scheme of having women
floor clerks; until then women had not been em-
ployed in hotels because people said hotel employment was not proper for refined women. Women

were not allowed to smoke, either. One night at the Plaza after dinner Mrs. Patrick Campbell lit a cigarette.

"Free!" she cried, dancing with rage, "you call this a free country. . . ."

"It is our rule, madam," she was told.

He was not the man to sympathize with a rule like that, but he knew that in the hotel business one must cater to the majority. Tact, he believes, is the main quality of a host; a hotel man is a professional host. He had learned this piece of wisdom from Sterry at the Plaza, which was the first metropolitan hotel Lucius Boomer had ever worked in. At the end of his second year he formed a partnership with an accountant named Merry. They took over the Nassau Hotel at Long Beach, a small place which was in debt even for its building bills, and made it pay; then they got the Taft at New Haven. The firm that had built the McAlpin was looking for someone to take it over; Boomer applied and was chosen. From that time on he was conspicuously successful.

Sterry—Merry—Sherry; they started a poem in the life of Lucius Boomer. Louis Sherry fitted into it. Lucius Boomer knew him—used to dine in his restaurant. One evening Sherry told him he was going to retire. Boomer offered to buy his name.

"What do you want it for?" Sherry asked. Boomer said he wanted it for a rhyme. He moved the restaurant to Park Avenue and opened a combination restaurant and candy store on Fifth Avenue at Fifty-eighth Street. More recently he opened another Sherry store on Fifth Avenue, at Thirty-fifth Street. He started another Sherry place in Paris. Frenchmen, tired of the Americans in the Ritz bar, go there to get ice-cream sodas. Mr. Boomer foresaw that they would. He foresaw, as a dollar-a-year man in the war, that the men quartered at the Hôtel du Louvre, which he was running for the A. E. F., would want pie for breakfast. He foresaw that he would make money if he ran the Willard, the Bellevue-Stratford, the Windsor, the Savarin restaurants. Mr. Coleman Dupont, who, as a large investor in the McAlpin, had met Boomer when the latter was managing that hotel, backed him in each of these ventures and in the Waldorf, and in the Sherry-Netherland. The Boomer-Dupont Holding Company owns all these hotels. Lucius Boomer is president of the company.

He has come a long way from the storeroom in the cellar of the Oriental Hotel. He has married, increased his large acquaintance; the passage of time has polished his tact and perfected his affability. He has a country place in Rockland County where he spends his summers with his wife and his two little children. When he is giving a friend lunch he usually goes to Sherry's, and if Sherry's is too far away he says, "Let's find a Savarin." In the winter he lives at the Sherry-Netherland. He has innovated or helped to innovate many improvements in the running of a hotel—a telephone switchboard on each floor, French, South American, Italian, German, Spanish employees assigned to take care of guests of those nationalities; a card credit system by which, as the checks come in, each item is placed under the guest's name so that when the guest wants to check out he can have "a bill in two minutes"—all the clerk has to do is add up the items. He has thought of ways to save waste; his bookkeeping taught him frugality.

His conservatism had become more marked as he grew older—no longer the purely professional conservatism of the hotel man, the tone that seems perpetually to be imparting a confidence, the slight turn of a plump, perfectly kept hand that indicates that there will be no trouble, no fuss; Lucius Boomer's conservatism had become intrinsic to his life and thought, so that it would have been almost impossible for him to make an unsafe speculation, a startling decision, or a speech that would cause gossip. His

life seemed to move on rubber heels, past many
doors, down a long, carpeted corridor.

He had come to a new enjoyment of living—an
enjoyment graver, perhaps, than the kind he had
liked in the days when Mrs. George Gould, falling
in with his tactful arrangements, made her return
to the stage, for charitable and publicity purposes,
in an amateur performance in the Hotel Plaza—
to the days when the McAlpin was filled with South
Americans who had been induced to come there by
the moving picture, advertising New York City and
the McAlpin Hotel, which Mr. Boomer had had
circulated through the Southern continent—the days
when the great Charles Rector was trying hard to
keep out of receivership the Hotel Claridge, which
Boomer eventually took over and ran till prohibition
made it profitless—the days when Louis Sherry still
owned the right to do business under his own name
and when the line of cab horses at Fifty-ninth Street
was twenty times as long as it is now.

And still something of the atmosphere of those
days clung about the dignified dark oak offices in
the old Waldorf, now demolished, where Lucius
Boomer worked on weekdays from ten to five, talking to his branch managers, or dictating to people
who have been guests in his hotels letters which—
like his personality—present behind their cordiality

that hint of propriety, of character, so looked for by people who are travelling.

All his life he has trained himself to think of effects in terms of figures; he has been successful because he has had luck, health, ambition, social talents, and the ability to combine imagination with brilliant bookkeeping. The Sherry-Netherland is his master production, the embodiment of everything he has learned. The groined ceilings, dressing rooms adjoining every bathroom, the built-in showers, the gold door knobs, triple-angled mirrors for shaving, quartered oak floors, and real travertine were the architect's idea, but the theory of the management of this hotel is Lucius Boomer's.

People are tired of living problems, he says. They are coming to see that an expert can solve these problems better than they can. In the apartments on the thirty-six floors of the Sherry-Netherland they can live in their own homes (homes which cost twenty thousand dollars a room to build) with their service, their comforts, supplied by him. He is proud of the Sherry-Netherland, yet, when one evening two years ago an excited agent telephoned him that the Sherry-Netherland was on fire, I don't believe he felt any particular emotion.

To the people who stopped their taxis on the drives in Central Park, who pressed in crowds down

Fifty-ninth Street, staring at the glow in the dark blue sky and at the dropping golden beams, the fire was an interesting and exciting spectacle. I think Lucius Boomer felt the same way about it. He knew that his contractor was fully covered by insurance, that this fire could at the worst only delay for a little while the realization of his plans. Service must go on. Always, in all his hotels, no matter what happened, it must go on.

THE PATRIARCH

THE PATRIARCH

LIKE the employees of all big companies, the people who work for Paramount-Famous-Lasky try to humanize their position by finding, or if necessary inventing, some trait in their president to which they can attach a nickname. They call Adolph Zukor "Pop." Many of them have never seen him, of course, but the name has more than a casual relevance; Zukor's paternal attitude is not limited to his own organization but is extended impartially to the industry at large. He thought up the present scheme whereby producing companies set up their own censorship; it was he who persuaded Will Hays to leave the Cabinet and come in as supercensor. As a further preventive of scandals in Hollywood, he started a school where young people on contract to Paramount were taught decorum. These pupils, selected by contests conducted in various colleges, learned how to conduct themselves before the camera and at the same time were given classes in sociology and English literature and lectured on the value of sobriety and an early bedtime.

Zukor is surprised when anybody criticizes his gestures for improving the social tone of the cinema as publicity schemes. Recently he told the head of his exploitation department that he was going to change the name of a picture which was about to be released and which was called *The Woman Who Needed Killing*. When the exploitation official protested that a great deal had already been spent advertising this title, Zukor got excited and behaved the way he always does when something has annoyed him—scratching his head and neck as though they were itching, as he walks rapidly up and down the carpet in front of the desk in his small, oak-paneled office on the eleventh floor of the Paramount Building. His mood, as usual, brought results. The first spreads were called in and others issued in which the original title was changed to *A Dangerous Woman*. Apparently something about saying that a woman needed killing seemed to Zukor a slur on womanhood, perhaps indirectly on mothers; as such it challenged the most important conviction of his character—his respect for the institution of the family.

For some time Zukor had kept close daily contact with his business, principally through the reports of his treasurers and occasional conferences on policy in the offices in Times Square. He was seen at the Hollywood studio so seldom that rumors grew up about him. It was said that, having made a huge fortune, he had retired, leaving most of his interests in charge of Benjamin Schulberg, manager of West coast production. There was a good deal of surprise when he appeared without warning in California and took active control of the affairs of the Paramount Company there.

He turned up at a time of excitement and confusion. Every company in Hollywood was reorganizing to produce dialogue pictures. Like other producers, Zukor did not know much about sound production except that there were enormous profits in it. He had to find out about it, and he conducted his investigations in person. Since he went around without the cortège of secretaries and publicity men usually attached to film magnates, he was not always recognized by the actors whom he watched at work or the technicians whom he cornered on production lots and questioned about costs.

His inconspicuousness is not due to lack of personality, but to his looking so much like hundreds of other men of his age and race. He is short, well knit, rough-skinned, with a crafty, energetic face and a cauliflower ear. He is fifty-seven years old, and the close-cut hair, bordering his high, round forehead, is turning gray. When he talks, his eyes look sharp and calculating, but at other times they have a placid, almost benevolent expression, as though continually replenished from some inner source of confidence. He looks taller sitting down than standing up, and it is easy to imagine him dining, as he sometimes does, with forty of his relatives, benign and cordial at the end of a long table.

That in business he is not regarded as the amiable character he appears to his large family may be owing to his early training in wholesale furs—a trade in which for a while he had a hard time. Before he learned how to stitch furs he worked for an upholsterer in Second Avenue but quit because he was so small that holding down sofa-springs while he tacked batting over them exhausted him. A lot of things had happened to him before he began to make money in the movies.

What is important in a story like his can be suggested by many somewhat isolated facts. Little Zukor coming over from Ricse, Hungary, when he was fifteen, with forty dollars sewed in his waistcoat . . . met at the dock by Hungarian cousins then living in Brooklyn . . . going to night school to learn English, particularly hard for all Hungarians because of the difference in word roots . . . learning to box, and getting one ear cauliflowered . . . learning to play baseball too, and being introduced one Sunday on the edge of a baseball lot to a dark-haired girl named Lottie Kaufman . . . falling in love with her at a pinochle game in her house . . . making profits in furs, clearing away his debts, and one day marrying Lottie Kaufman in the synagogue in the presence of all her relatives, a numerous congregation of dark-eyed, able-bodied people. After his marriage Zukor lived in the Bronx across the street from another furrier whose round head with its thick eyebrows and mustache looked like a baseball to which twists of horsehair had been glued. This furrier, whose name was Marcus Loew, went into the theater business, and Zukor invested some money in the company he formed.

For some time the returns on the Loew stock kept the Zukors prosperous, although his other investments brought in meager returns. Adolph had sold his fur business and bought a downtown penny arcade, which he sold a few months later without making any profit. He invested in a sideshow project called "Hale's Tours," in which a crude movie of Mont Blanc was shown in a gallery which rocked and swayed to simulate the movement of an observation car. His partner, William A. Brady, was already well known as a producer. Zukor had met him while he owned the penny arcade. Hale's Tours made money at first, then got into debt and did not recoup its losses even when Zukor added to the travelogue a cinema with a real story—*The Great Train Robbery*. Eventually the partners sold out Hale's Tours but continued their association in other enterprises. Investing in a small way in various of Brady's schemes, Zukor spent most of his time managing a movie theater in Fourteenth Street.

Zukor ran the Fourteenth Street Theater for seven years. He used his spare time to find out how pictures were made. He hung around the studios of the Biograph Company, then one of the leading producers, asking questions and watching how things were done. Unlike Brady, he thought that there was more chance of making money in pictures than in productions for the legitimate stage. During this period as an exhibitor he was making plans to produce pictures himself. When he was ready to form a company he invited Brady to come in with him. Brady refused because he thought the venture was too speculative, but Zukor went ahead with his plans just the same. Without a financial backer, with no experience in making pictures, without even a license from the "trust" of ten companies that controlled the existing patents on cameras and films, he introduced his new company to the trade by presenting Sarah Bernhardt in a French cinema called *Queen Elizabeth,* at the Lyceum Theater, in July, 1912.

When asked now to explain his success, Zukor generally says that he rode a tide. He has also been known to tell young men that there are no large profits in the moving-picture business. These statements are not inspired so much by modesty as by a superstitious unwillingness to analyze what has turned out well. As a matter of fact, Famous Players succeeded because it was founded on a policy that had been thought out beforehand with the greatest care and even brilliance. Up to that time producers had not advertised their actors and had paid them as little as they could. Zukor decided that no matter what it cost he would get people famous on the legitimate stage to work for him. One night on a scratch pad he wrote a slogan: "Famous Players in Famous Plays."

From a tiny but fierce trade war waged by a group of unstable little companies, the cinema industry developed in the next four years like a plant in one of those educational films in which growth-processes usually occupying months take place before your eyes in a few minutes. During the first six months of operation in 1912 Zukor's company was on the verge of bankruptcy three times—twice on a pay day—occasions when somehow or other he managed to raise loans—and once when the studio burned down. By 1916 he was leading his field and

his assets were so fluid that he could not tell whether
they were worth ten million or twenty-five million
dollars. He broke the so-called trust and merged
Famous Players with Jesse Lasky's independent corporation with himself as president of the new company and Lasky as vice president in charge of
production. Famous Players-Lasky bought the great
distributing company, Paramount, and then the
theaters—now about seven hundred of them—belonging to the Publix string. The talked-of merger
with Warner Brothers involves a total of twenty-
four hundred motion-picture theaters, and envisages
the largest chain in the United States. Before Mary
Pickford left him to go with United Artists, Zukor
had increased her pay from twenty thousand dollars
to a quarter of a million a year; from producing
eight or ten pictures annually he had come to produce more than a hundred and fifty. S. R. Kent,
whom he raised from a humble position to general
managership of his combined companies, makes
about a hundred and fifty thousand a year; Benjamin Schulberg, who came to Famous Players as
publicity man, is now in charge of West coast production at about two hundred thousand; Walter
Wanger has charge of Eastern production at almost
as much. Although he pays sums of this kind to
officials working for him, Zukor for a long time

kept himself on a pittance of fifty thousand a year
so as to save money for the company.

One thing that helped his success is his habit
of enforcing his own judgment in matters of cash
business but subordinating it in artistic problems
to people whom he considers better qualified than he
is. He was one of the first producers to hire pro-
fessors to advise his directors on historical settings.
When he has to decide himself some question involving taste, like the decoration of the Paramount
Theater, he is never confident. On the afternoon before the theater was opened he stood in the lobby
looking speculatively at the fountain, the nymphs in
ormolu, and the Gargantuan chandeliers.

"Maybe it's not good enough; we don't know yet."

His doubts ended when Otto Kahn appeared and
told him he liked the decorations, a statement that
encouraged Zukor to make one of his rare public
speeches. He talks the English he learned on the fur
bench. His favorite phrases are "first class," "high
class," "cash on the dot," and "fifty-fifty."

An English author whom he met at dinner told
him that the greatest book in the language was *The
Mayor of Casterbridge*. Zukor, whose reading is
generally confined to the plots of films, had a synopsis made of Hardy's story, read it and decided that
it would make a high-class production. He had it

adapted for film production several times, but the adaptations never satisfied him, and he is still looking for one that will.

His instinct for finding picture talent in odd places has led him to make mistakes and at times to accept rebuffs. When Lindbergh flew to Paris, Zukor, who was also there, showed a paper containing the story to one of his directors.

"Marvelous," said the director, who was looking at the text.

Zukor was looking at Lindbergh's photograph.

"You said it!" he exclaimed. "Perfect! He has —natural—a perfect face for pictures."

He made Lindbergh several offers and for some time refused to believe that he couldn't hire anyone in the world for Paramount. His failure left him with the belief that he had not offered the aviator enough money.

He insists on an efficiency in domestic life corresponding to that of his business. When showing visitors around his big place near Nyack he surprises them with his knowledge of farming methods. He usually knows how many quarts of milk his thoroughbred cattle are giving each week. The fields around the farm and the big lawns of his estate have been modeled into a full-length golf course which he sometimes plays under a hundred and ten.

When one of the Schencks beat him he began taking regular lessons from Leo Diegel, whom he engaged as his private instructor at ten thousand dollars a year. Even his Irish caretaker became inoculated with the spirit of efficiency and invented an arrangement of shotguns rigged at each cellar window to go off if burglars tried to get in. To everyone's surprise the thing went off one night and killed a man.

This country mansion is really two houses—a "day" house of dining rooms and drawing rooms, big but simply furnished, and a "night" house containing nothing but bedrooms. His week-end guests, sometimes twenty or thirty, go from the day to the night house on a covered path. He does more entertaining in the country than in town. Usually the Zukors move to Nyack early in the spring from their apartment in the Savoy-Plaza, and they stay late in the fall; Adolph and his son, Eugene, who is "assistant to the President," go to business on working days by yacht. Adolph is a Mason, a Lamb, and a Friar, but he seldom takes part in club activities; if he is not giving a party himself he likes to go to the movies with his family or to play bridge with such friends as the Schencks or Felix Kahler or Jesse Lasky. He is good at bridge but never plays with anyone who does not know him well, having found that strangers do not seem to understand his passionate interest in winning. He used to play with Marcus Loew a lot, not always amicably. A friend who invited them both to a party was amazed to hear shouts in the bridge room followed by the crash of a table falling. Loew came out, followed by Zukor, who was trembling with rage. After some discussion the host cleared up a point about a certain club lead, and the antagonists, still refusing to speak to each other, picked up the table and went on with the rubber.

This excitability finds expression in other, less childish, ways. The same sentimentality that makes him cry, so that he is sometimes caught in tears when the lights go on in his private projection room after the showing of a picture, leads him also to give money away in odd kinds of charity. He sends, for instance, a private allowance to almost half the inhabitants of the Hungarian village where he was born and pays an agent in Budapest to see how the money is used and to recommend to him other people worthy of help. He seems to feel responsible for these people, and on his visits to Ricse he asks to hear their troubles and hands out money prodigally.

He is responsible also for a good many things which have no direct part in his business or his life.

As virtual controller of one of the most important organizations in the film business, this little man who was too small to push down the sofa springs, the Hungarian immigrant, the furrier, the theater owner, exerts an influence on popular thought and culture so extensive and powerful that it cannot be accurately appraised. Through the pictures produced in his name, he invades the imaginations of millions of people, influencing their manners, their taste in clothes and haircuts, and even—thanks to the sound device—their speech.

Accepting this power as an inevitable part of his business, he neither uses it for idealistic betterment nor—according to his standards—degrades it. As for business, he subordinates that to nothing at all except, possibly, his family. Usually impatient of the slightest interruptions of his routine in the office, he once kept a conference of a thousand branch managers waiting for an hour because his daughter had brought his grandson to see him. As you would expect, he took the baby into the conference room and introduced him to the boys. Like his concern for cinema morals and his satisfaction when one of the actresses working for him gets married, his feeling for family shows you a pleasant side of his character. What he owns, controls, he has made part of a tribal house. He is a sort of patriarch, and at those times when he sits down to dinner with forty people of his house he must feel, looking down the table, that the promises of good harvests and many descendants made to the fathers in the old time have come out right for him.

SPREAD EAGLE

SPREAD EAGLE

WHEN William F. Carey became president of the Madison Square Garden Corporation after Tex Rickard's death, people who knew him could not understand why he had taken the job. It certainly seemed odd that a man who had been busy all his life building railroads and canals should abruptly become interested in promoting. Those who had always made their living from sport were puzzled too, and for a while few of them could figure Carey out as a personality.

One thing that made it hard for them to know how to take Carey was the suddenness of his change from treasurer of the Garden to being a promoter himself. His arrival in Miami to boss the preparations for the Stribling-Sharkey fight was the first personal link between professional sport and the forces of big business that had functioned importantly but remotely behind Rickard's enterprises. Carey had a problem to face right away; the papers were panning the fight, and there was a general feeling that it might be a failure. Carey issued the optimistic statements expected of a promoter, but did not hesitate to admit in private that he was skeptical of the way things were going. He explained his attitude by comparing the situation in Miami with something that had happened to him in the past. He told how he had dug a railroad tunnel through a mountain at some frontier. He had no way of telling what he would find as the tunnel got deeper: perhaps rock, perhaps water. . . . He drew out the figure, using it to illustrate that promoting a fight was a construction job in which you never knew what to expect.

Why he translates difficulties into engineering terms before sizing them up is explained by what he has done. He was born in 1878 on a farm near Hoosick Falls, New York. He had three brothers and three sisters. His father worked in a stone quarry; his mother managed the farm. Not wanting to be a farmer, he left for Colorado one day with eleven dollars he had made out of his own cabbage patch. He was sixteen then. In Colorado he drove a team for fifteen dollars a week. The railroad construction in which he was taking so humble a part attracted him; he got to be a foreman, but quit to go down to Panama in 1904. In two years of work on the Canal he had risen from bossing a gang of Negroes to general superintendent of all steam-shovel operations in Culebra Cut. He could not afford to stay long in this position at the salary he was getting. He had attracted attention as a builder of extraordinary ability; he took contracts in other parts of the country, and at the end of 1906 he left Panama to go back to railroad building. Forming his own construction company, he worked on sections of the Great Northern, the Northern Pacific, the Grand Trunk Pacific, the Canadian Northwestern, the Wisconsin Central, and the Chicago & Northwestern. By 1916 he had central offices in Wall Street and branch companies working all over the world, making canals, dams, railroads, bridges, highways, factories. He formed his connections with the Garden Corporation by contracting with Hayden, Stone & Company to put up the arena in Eighth Avenue; later he took so much stock in the new company that he was made treasurer.

A construction expert is not a bureaucrat but a master workman whose employees fulfill literally the position implied by the word "help." Running the business concerns of his companies, Carey had become a millionaire; as director of operations in the field he has attracted a kind of loyalty that nobody gets but the most talented natural leaders. One of his old foremen, now head of an independent construction company, becomes angry whenever he hears Carey called a promoter.

"You don't know anything about him. To a man

like that Madison Square Garden is no more than a dog kennel."

It is hard to understand why, although reputed to be one of the most important contractors in the country, his name was scarcely known to the public until last year. One reason for this is that he considers publicity unnecessary in the building business —has never given out an interview about himself, and will seldom read a clipping in which he is mentioned. Another is that his activities have been carried on mostly in uncivilized parts of the world where there was no one to stare at them and ask questions. From various continents and outposts have come back records of his accomplishments, bordered with the anecdotes that compose the Carey legend.

When he got his first promotion in Panama he grew a beard so as to look older. The precaution was probably unnecessary—you can't reasonably think that he ever looked juvenile. He has big features and small eyes that are attentive and expressive but always slightly clouded. His skin is weather-beaten and deeply lined, and his mud-colored hair is unevenly dusted with gray. He is big and thick-set, but unusually active and graceful; he shakes hands lightly, and speaks in a low voice. Although he has never affected the loud and genial fellowship which, combined with chicanery, is a tradition of the fight business, he knows how to behave in his new environment.

One of the items in his legend is the fact that he was once a sort of king in a city of his own with a territory about twice as big as Belgium. That was in 1912, in British Columbia. Winter had forced his company to stop work while laying out the Grand Trunk Pacific and Carey decided to wait for spring without leaving the job. In a sprawling city of tar-paper shacks several thousand workmen tried to keep out the cold. They dug ditches around their houses and banked the earth against the bottom of the walls. Carey lived at the end of the city street in a shack that was smaller than the rest because he lived alone. Since work on the railroad was impossible he thought out ways to improve conditions in his city. He built a power house and put in electric light; he built a city hall. As a final gesture he even sent back to the coast for sheets and pillowcases and distributed them to the railroad builders who had been sleeping for months in dirty blankets. When a deputation came up to his house to thank him for the linen, he passed it off with a king's air. How did a human being sleep? Not in a sour straw bunk. That might be all right for a jackass; a human being had sheets and pillowcases.

Before spring came a civilization had been improvised in the frontier settlement. The rumor of it spread and greatly increased his prestige. He spent several years building the Grand Trunk, and each year Carey City, rising in a new site along the route of operations, grew more elaborate. There were fellows in the camp who would not hesitate to commit a murder when a fight got started, but someone who had been there said afterward that if Carey had lost his pocketbook with a thousand dollars in it, and one of the construction hands had picked it up, the finder would have brought it back to Carey. The British Columbians had a nickname for him. They called him an eagle, comparing him, for the sake of emphasis, with a foreman whom they disliked.

"Jensen is a pudding, but Carey is an eagle."

As king of his state Carey was lawmaker and magistrate; he decided quarrels and adjusted penalties. His success gave him courage for new responsibilities. When the Grand Trunk Pacific was finished he showed more and more his preference for work that other contractors had turned down because of its difficulties. He explained that he took such jobs because the returns were in proportion to the risks, but I think the difficulties themselves challenged and satisfied him. He proved this definitely when he was working on the Northern Pacific, near Paradise, Montana.

It was what railroad men call a steam-shovel job, ordinarily easy enough, but hard in this instance because there was no practical way of getting the machinery where it was needed. To take it apart and pack it on mules would have taken a long time. Carey decided to leave it whole and float it down the Yellowstone River on scows. He had the scows built, but when the time came to start he could not find a crew for them. It was generally believed that the tricky, dangerous river, with its rapids and uncharted rocks and sand bars, made his scheme impractical. When he announced that he was going to take the scows down himself people said that his machinery would be lost and that he and anyone with him would be killed.

He started early in the morning. Some cowboys and a few of his own men stood on the bank to see him off. Carey took the stern oar of one of the scows and told four volunteers who had come·on board with him to cast off. Although he had never steered a boat before and knew little about the eccentric currents of the river, he somehow avoided an accident. It took him four hours to get his equipment where he wanted to land it.

This adventure saved him six months of tedious

work and a lot of money, but you are still left wondering why he chose it. Evidently he had balanced the delay and safety of travel by land against the advantages of the river and chosen the dangerous way because, if it could be managed, it was more his style.

In 1915 he had an idea that China needed railroads and went there to look things over. He secured a contract from the Chinese government and, with three thousand coolies on the job, put a line through Manchuria. During the war he tunneled through a mountain range in Washington to tap an untouched spruce forest, and put up the biggest sawmills in the world to make spruce timber into lumber for airplanes. He had just finished his contract when the armistice was signed.

Moving his private office from Wall Street to Madison Square Garden does not mean that he has retired from building operations. His construction companies—the Sims-Carey Railway & Canal Company, and W. F. Carey & Company—are busy in different parts of the world; he is president of a company that mines and exports phosphates from South America, and is a partner of the separate construction corporation of Kennedy & Carey. He is now building a big dam in Vermont, a forty-one-million-dollar railroad across the Andes for the

government of Bolivia, and a new airport, planned
as the biggest in the world, on the meadows behind
Newark. Builders who have worked with him since
his days in Panama, and others whom he has trained
himself, or picked out for their knowledge of construction methods, manage these projects so that
he does not have to bother with details; he decides
on costs and matters of policy and receives reports
on the various jobs in his simply furnished offices in
the Forty-ninth Street side of the Garden.

I think that promoting sport interests him as
much as anything else he is doing. It is new, stren-
uous, and entertaining; it has qualities that he began
to miss in the increasing prosperity of his other
business. Sitting down to dinner in his house in
Miami with a company of active and retired prize
fighters and their associates was a novelty that presented some problems to his wife. The guests liked
to come to the table without their coats, and for
some time Mrs. Carey tried to arrive at a tactful
way of correcting this without hurting anyone's
feelings. She found an opportunity one evening
when, as usual, everyone had come in without a
coat except Carey himself. He looked neat and
proper, but Mrs. Carey amazed the table by asking
him mildly to go and brush his hair. As he left the
room the guests took the hint and came back but-

toning their coats. After this, the dinners at the Careys' house were conducted with befitting decorum.

After the Stribling-Sharkey fight had been brought off successfully in spite of all forebodings to the contrary, Carey came North and a few weeks later gave a party for the Ranger hockey team. He has given one of these parties annually since the Garden was built, and they get better every year. Such hockey players as Bill Cook and Frank Boucher sometimes tell how Carey took them each by an arm and led them up to a bare and apparently solid wall, and how the wall suddenly rolled up to the ceiling, revealing a long, shiny bar, and pyramids of colored bottles and bright glasses, and three bartenders at work. Carey's penthouse apartment in East Sixty-ninth Street has other interesting features. There is, for instance, a radio set with an extension in every room, plugged into the wall like a light, which can be turned on by pressing a button. If you don't like the tune you press another button that switches off the radio and turns on an electric victrola. Buttons are set so that you can reach them while lying in the bathtub. The installation cost sixteen thousand dollars. Carey likes things like this better than most antiques, but is fond of a collection of old Spanish silver that he found in South America. Sometimes he takes the silver out of its cabinet and runs his fingers over the worn surfaces.

During the summer he spends part of his time on the place he built several years ago on Center Island, facing Oyster Bay. He has sometimes finished a railroad in the time it took him to get his house done. Fast and exacting when working on contract, concentrating on the main problem and filling in details afterward, he built his own house in an entirely different way. Instead of insisting on adherence to a definite, preconceived plan, he supervised and altered details himself, and even took suggestions from his architect and from local country builders. His land includes a long stretch of waterfront near the Seawanhaka Club. A launch and a couple of sailboats nod at their moorings off the end of his dock. Yachting is the hobby of this man who was born inland and has worked on plains, swamps, and mountains all his life.

In early spring a year ago he leased the Polo Grounds and the Yankee Stadium for fight shows. He spent a lot of time himself making deals with the fighters he wanted to get or who had been suggested to him by his matchmaker. Before each outdoor show he went to the grounds early and supervised personally the arrangements that were being made for handling the crowds.

He has been known to take fifteen or twenty guests to a fight. If the evening is pleasant he likes to motor down to Oyster Bay; sometimes he finds his son or his young daughter giving a party. His children are slighter, smaller-boned than he, as though bred in a different country, under quieter skies and a milder sun.

There is no pattern for pioneers. A few stand up, lonely in any generation, who find cities no place for them and so beleaguer the world's last frontiers. Carey may get out of sport the kind of excitement that he, and others like him, building the machines for civilization, have to some extent eliminated, but this contradiction, if it exists, does not bother him; he seems to have a good time at the ringside in ball parks on summer nights.

PANDORA AND THE DOCTOR

PANDORA AND THE DOCTOR

NOT many millionaires get up at seven o'clock to see customers. Not many corporation heads stay awake all night, now and then, to work, nor are they in the habit of getting up, when they are called, from the theater, from a dinner party, to go where they are wanted on business. Surgeons do these things, for all of which they deserve little credit, perhaps, except the honor that belongs impersonally to the trade they have chosen and to each of its company of unhasty artisans who earn their living, like carpenters, by the wisdom of their hands.

Like many eminent New Yorkers, Dr. John Frederick Erdmann came from the Middle West. He has made New York his habitat, and his colleagues speak of "Erdmann of New York" in a tone of respect they use for only a few of the very greatest American surgeons, such men as Lahey of Boston, Dever of Philadelphia, Finney of Baltimore, Crile of Cleveland, Judd and the brothers Mayo of Rochester, and Rowan of Iowa City. Dr. Erdmann has realized most of his professional and social ambitions; he has a good many of both. In person he is a compact, rather stomachy short man, beautifully tailored; across the room his face looks fat, but when you come close it seems thinner; and sometimes you see that he is tired with the distant, habitual weariness that gives doctors their dignity. He never drinks or does calisthenics; and if he gets any exercise it is by walking through the wards.

Once he was seen leaving a professional banquet with a cigar in his mouth; when the doorman of the Waldorf looked at him he threw it abruptly away, nor has he at any other time been known to smoke. His speech is notoriously brusque, a relic possibly left over from the time before he was known, a time of which the story still clings to him in shreds, lending him a suggestion of dim drama. You would want to know his story if you saw him operate some afternoon at the Post-Graduate Hospital, but he would not want you to know it, because, like most other medical men, he dreads publicity. And in writing of Dr. Erdmann we are taking liberties, perhaps, with the profession that more than any other makes an honest effort to avoid self-advertising.

There, on a singularly noisy corner of Second Avenue, where the nurses in their pale starch are forever stepping back and forth from the hospital door to the brick Training School across the street,

his arrival causes a sensation. He drives up in a
blue Packard and nods to the doorman. Instantly
the news travels down the long antiseptic-
smelling corridors. "John Erdmann is here,"
the nurses say to their patients, and then they tell
you what his schedule is. To-day he will do five
abdominal operations, including one on the girl they
brought in Thursday in such bad condition. Sometimes it is not five but nine or ten—once it was fourteen abdominal operations. He works with amazing
rapidity; long practice has developed the natural
deftness of his fingers; and then, too, he has deliberately schooled himself to ambidexterity. An operation that might take a less experienced surgeon
twenty minutes takes him four; his bleak punctilios
with scalpel and artery clips have become so much
a formula that he does not have to think about them
and so is the more ready to deal with emergencies.
Speed is all in the patient's favor; if the incision is
quickly closed the wasting of blood and strength
will be proportionately brief.

Usually it is after he has left the operating theater
that he begins to visit among the ladies and gentlemen who lie in bed. He looks at the chart. He
asks a question or two to assure himself of the
patient's condition; then, usually, he makes a joke.
His jokes are nothing much to repeat, but they have

an amazing effect in a sick-room; most of them are
metropolitan in character, but a few—like the one
about Murphy and the fireman's wife, or the one
about the peddler with the harelip—have a smack of
the mid-West; it is possible that he brought these
with him when he arrived, one September day in
1884, to take up his studies at the Bellevue Medical
College. Finding himself, in due course, a doctor, he
took an office on Lexington Avenue and put a sign
out—no modest placard, peeping above a soiled win-
dow-ledge—but a resounding painted sign that
swung upon a staple:

JOHN ERDMANN, M. D.

"You could see it," said one of his colleagues,
"for ten blocks." John Erdmann was twenty-three
when he began to practise; pretty soon he was able
to move to a better office on West Thirty-fourth
Street, and fifteen years after the appearance of that
sign he bought his present house at 60 West Fifty-
second Street and installed himself and his success
against a permanent and civilized background.

The years between were dignified by effort,
steady progress, a laboriously and slowly acquired
knowledge of surgery and men. Even in Chillicothe,
Ohio, where, against the background of a family

business in merchant tailoring, he grew up and went to high school, he had been ambitious; Chillicothe and Lexington Avenue were both well behind him when, at thirty, he married, but from the fasts and vigils of those early years he extracted the talisman that brought him to the bedsides of the great.

Most doctors who in later life build up large practices among people of fashion have, even at the beginning, some entrée into the polite world. John Erdmann worked among clerks and truckmen and small tradespeople. He worked fast. He said what he had to say in frank, and sometimes in Elizabethan, terms. And when his rapidly growing reputation as an operating surgeon brought him into contact with people of larger incomes he made no changes in this manner of his, and the manner, giving his natural abilities the accolade of individuality, motioned him on to success.

Did he subtly realize that prosperous patients found his brusqueness a novelty and liked it? Did he perceive that these people, unaccustomed to being barked at when they lay abed, took his blunt speech as a sort of tonic, or did he simply clip his words because he wanted to save time? It is hard to say. He knew, to be sure, that his Third Avenue patients had no respect for a doctor who did not bully them; he had no time to suit his manner to prosperity, and it remained what it had always been, hectoring and brusque and distantly jocose.

"All I know, madam," he barked at a celebrated hostess who had shown an unwillingness to call things by their names, "all I know is that you have a thousand-dollar operation under your gown."

Bluntness is not a universally admired virtue, and from time to time people have taken offense at the brevities of John Erdmann. But generally he is liked, accepted, for what he is—an efficient man with a winning personality and a genuine talent for plain speech. He has not lost touch with his first patients, butchers and apothecaries; they still ask his advice, for they know that his fees—from three hundred to twenty thousand dollars—are infinitely flexible. He does a large amount of free work. One evening, starting for his Easthampton place from the Post Graduate, he noticed a laborer doubled up on a curbstone. "Pain in da bell'," the sufferer explained. Dr. Erdmann, with the help of his chauffeur, lifted the man into the tonneau, drove him back to the hospital, and removed his appendix before starting, once more, for Easthampton. Events of this kind not infrequently interrupt his summer week-ends; even in Easthampton the telephone rings and he will start back to New York. Medical men have hinted that such behavior is not good for him, but John Erdmann has that trace of impatience with medical doctors which more or less characterizes all good surgeons. A patient whom he had examined paused at the door for a last question. "What does my report mean when it says 'blood pressure alarmingly low'?"

Dr. Erdmann waved his arm.

"Don't know," he said, "nobody knows. Five years ago they wouldn't give me life insurance because I had low blood pressure, and now look at me!—doing more work than anybody else in town."

He seldom leaves the city. Once a year, in August, he takes two weeks off and goes fishing in Maine. He spends the rest of his time, except week-ends, in town, listening to the whispers of Pandora.

Pandora is made of brass. Her sly immortal silhouette emerges from the cream-colored stone of the Erdmann house in Fifty-second Street; her middle contains a bell push. Inside, a lamp on a Florentine table blooms quietly in the big hall that does duty as a waiting room. At the end of the hall is another door, beside which, in an alcove, sit two nurses. A buzzer, pressed by a dim finger lost behind that inner door, rasps briefly, and one of the nurses gets up and ushers a patient through the door. The buzzer rasps again, and the nurse calls the name of another patient. Again the buzzer and now

a third patient disappears through the door. None
have come out. Are they, you wonder, sitting in con-
clave, pouring out the story of their symptoms in a
sort of prayer meeting?

A trip inside is reassuring. There are three offices
behind the central, inner door—John Erdmann's
study, and, to left and right, a pair of examining
rooms. He receives patients successively in all three,
pressing a buzzer whenever he is ready for a new
case.

All of the partitions are relatively soundless, but
visitors in the study can hear, from the closed booths
on each side, occasional strange, peremptory cate-
chisms. A Firm Voice: "D'ye vomit?" Murmurous
response.

A Firm Voice: "Any headache? And pains at
night? Any . . . ?" The nurse shuts the door

For the last four years John Erdmann has performed an average of a thousand operations a year.
He has come to the top of his profession. Surgeons,
to be sure, are not graded like tennis players, but
if they were John Erdmann would be well in the
upper flight—anyway, in the American first ten.
He works almost as hard to keep his place as he did
to get it.

A list of his patients is a directory of directors.
They keep him busier than ever the tradesmen did

who saw his sign on Lexington Avenue. From eight
to ten he pays calls; from ten to two he receives
patients; from three to five he is at the Post Graduate. And after that, wherever he is, he has to be
somewhere else in a minute. Patients in three con-
sulting rooms; operations in three hospitals, and always his blue Packard waiting outside to take him
away. His day and his life are, after all, only typical
of those of every eminent surgeon whose practice has
grown so big that it has set up vibrations around
him. He may grow tired, sometimes, of such perpetual motion, but he has unloosed a force that
whirls on, bearing with it, beyond his own resistance,
this blunt-shaped, short-talking, efficient carpenter
of life and death, John Erdmann, M. D.

A DOWNTOWN GABRIEL

A DOWNTOWN GABRIEL

PARISHIONERS of Dean Randolph Ray, rector of the Little Church Around the Corner, say that if he had not been a clergyman he could have been an actor. You could make the same statement of many other clerics, for persons of dramatic ability have been and still are so numerous in his profession that they have come to constitute a traditional type. As applied to Dean Ray, however, the observation is not superficial. He speaks like an actor, goes to the theater often, has acted in amateur shows, and is the friend of many stage people.

I don't want to make too much of this. Another quality just as characteristic as his taste for the theater was summed up by a young woman who was taken by some friends to a dinner party in the rectory of the Little Church Around the Corner without having previously met the Dean.

"As soon as I saw him, I knew that we were going to have a good dinner."

It is easy to see how Dean Ray gave his guest this idea. His bearing and appearance are not ascetic. He is tall, plump, bland, and dignified; he has thin

hair, a short nose, small blue eyes, and a long upper
lip. In any gathering, a certain intimacy in his manner softens the more exacting dignity distinguish-
ing, on Sundays, his ringing aphorisms from the
pulpit. During the day much of his time is taken up
in marrying the couples who come to his church in
rapid succession, yet he investigates so carefully
all marriages at which he is asked to officiate that
eloping couples joined by him have as much prestige
as if they had been married more formally, uptown.
For this and other reasons it is said in church circles
that no rector was ever better fitted than Dean Ray
to uphold the social importance of the Little Church
Around the Corner.

Dean Ray's wife, the grand-daughter of Dean
Hoffman, one of the most prominent New York prel-
ates of the 'nineties, was a friend of the daughter of
the late Dr. Houghton, the Dean's predecessor in the
downtown parish. While Ray was in the seminary
he met Dr. Houghton and attended his services, and
decided at the time that Dr. Houghton's parish was
a desirable and attractive one. He confided this
opinion to one or two clergymen who also knew
Houghton, and who may have said a word to him in
Ray's behalf, for one day, on a train leaving some
religious conference, the Bishop of western Mis-

souri told the Dean that Dr. Houghton had picked
him as his successor.

It is often in some such way as this that important
Episcopal parishes are passed from one man to another. Ray was familiar with the method, but he
could hardly have expected its successful results—
anyway, not so soon. The only son of a Mississippi
cotton planter, he had gone to Emory and Henry
College in Virginia and then come North to study
some profession suitable for a gentleman—he was
not sure what. He thought at first it might be medicine, but an afternoon spent at Bellevue with some
fellows from Emory and Henry who were internes
there put an end to that idea. The possibility of
working in a place filled with the physical details
of suffering and death frightened and shocked him.
For a while he studied law at Columbia, where he
joined a clique of artistic young men who were
inspired with admiration for the late Professor
Brander Matthews. Matthews was nice to him.
When Ray decided that the difficulty and dullness of
law made it, though cleaner, almost as unpleasant as
medicine, the Professor gave him a letter to the editor of one of Munsey's magazines. Ray became a
writer and worked for Mr. Munsey for a while
and later for the Brooklyn *Eagle* and a clothing trade

paper called *Nugent's Bulletin,* writing whatever the
editors of these various publications suggested to
him in the way of fillers and special articles.

During this time of varying and not very successful pursuits he had acquired an interest in the
theater. He made friends with actors and spent his
holidays with them and himself acted in amateur
theatricals. No marked change affected this interest
even when he withdrew from Brooklyn journalism
to study for orders in the General Theological Seminary. Apparently his sudden decision to become a
clergyman was not motivated by any crisis in his
own life. He had been thinking for quite a while that
the church would be a more satisfying profession
than those he had been trying. Reading some of
Browning's poetry about worldly churchmen who
made converts and inspired faith in spite of their
faults made him decide that even without inspiration he might become an able worker in a figurative
vineyard. His new ambition did not mean retirement
from the world. While he studied at the seminary he
shared two rooms with an artist in the Hotel
Grenoble and cultivated an English accent with a
view—he now facetiously admits—to its effect in
his sermons. At Christmas time the seminary students gave a play and dressed him up in a sheet
and wings as Gabriel.

Not being able to go to the theater any more or act in amateur plays was one of the things that made life hard for him after he had been ordained, and, in due course, sent to Bryan, Texas, as chaplain of an agricultural college. For some reason he had never tried to act professionally—perhaps because he did not want to spoil his pleasure in the stage by making it responsible for another disappointment. He had, however, taken part in undergraduate musical comedy at Columbia and later been a Greek soldier, without pay, in *Euripides* with the Ben Greet Players. There were no such activities in Bryan. The students there talked about pigs, cattle, and manure. They got bored if you read them a sermon; you had to reel it off from notes, as though you were making it up.

By degrees he made the students at Bryan get used to him. It was the hardest thing he had ever done, and it would have been hard for a smarter man than Randolph Ray. For a long time his only contact with his former interests was the occasional visits of stock companies to a town near Bryan. Whenever one of these shows visited the town, the chaplain of the veterinaries' college drove over to the theater and invited the actors to have dinner with him. Meanwhile his reputation as a preacher was growing. He was transferred to the Cathedral

of St. Matthew in Dallas and given the title of
"Dean" which he still uses. During the war there
was an aviation camp at Dallas to which, among
other recruits, came some actors. He persuaded a
few of them to come to the social affairs he organized, and one night Earl Carroll directed an amateur
show in his parish house.

By 1923, when he got his appointment to the Little
Church Around the Corner, he was already fairly
well known.

He took his new duties in the light of a reward
which God had sent him to compensate for the difficult years away from the East. There was a superstition in the New York parish that the rectors of
the Little Church Around the Corner died as soon as
they had appointed their successors. By a coincidence, it worked out again. Dr. Houghton died three
days after Ray's arrival, and the new rector was
left alone to marry the couples who came to the
church at all hours. At first the romantic atmosphere
of elopements invited his sense of the dramatic, and
he performed wedding ceremonies rapidly and without asking questions beforehand, like a rector in an
eighteenth-century play. After one or two incidents
in which parents protested against this method he
adopted his present caution. If he suspects that bride
or groom is under age, he calls mothers or guardians

on the telephone, insisting on written consent or on the presence of some member of the family. Sometimes, of course, a runaway débutante or college boy manages to fool him, as last year, when a girl introduced as her uncle a dignified sunburned man who turned out later to have been the captain of her father's yacht. In 1928 six hundred couples were turned away from his church, but more than two thousand were married there. One day when his assistants were sick Ray joined thirty-nine pairs by himself.

Before Ray's rectorship the pastors of the Little Church Around the Corner had obeyed the rules of the Church against marrying divorced people but had conveyed the impression that, outside of this, they would marry almost anyone. The church had become a center for marriages in 1870, when a now famous incident brought it to public attention.

Few people nowadays have not heard how Joseph Jefferson went to a Fifth Avenue prelate to arrange the funeral of a fellow actor and how— when he was told that the Fifth Avenue church did not bury actors, but that a little one around the corner did—Joseph Jefferson raised his hand and in his best dramatic manner invited God to bless the little church around the corner. This episode created so much sentiment for the church that such actors as Amelia Bingham, Maurice Barrymore, Edwin Booth, and Richard Mansfield became parishioners. Rich people donated chapels, pictures, and stained-glass windows. Between 1870 and 1920 fifty thousand couples were married there, and by the time Ray took Dr. Houghton's place the yearly average had risen from one thousand to two thousand and is still increasing.

Officiating at so many weddings brought a problem into the Dean's life which up to that time he had not considered. Every wedding meant a fee for him—from one dollar to five hundred, depending on the groom's means and on what he felt like giving: sometimes a crumpled bill, sometimes silver, sometimes gold pieces in a special chamois bag slipped deftly into the clergyman's hand at parting. Although these fees at the Little Church amounted to twenty-five thousand dollars a year—an average of twelve and a half dollars per wedding—they presented no problem to Ray until one day a waiter in a restaurant observed to him that the best-dressed people gave the smallest tips and asked him if he had not found this so in the clerical profession. . . . Tips? This odd definition of the fees offered and received so undemonstratively was emphasized a little later when a rich gentleman who was chief mourner at a funeral pressed a folded bill against

Ray's palm as he shook hands with him at the end of the obsequies. It was a conventional thing to do, but the chief mourner added unconventionally, in a tone clearly audible to all the other mourners, "Buy yourself some cigars."

Ray blushed furiously but took the bill. Later he sent it back. The chief mourner then forwarded the same amount by check with a letter in which he apologized for his inconsiderate phrase about the cigars and telling the Dean to use the money for anything at all. Ray kept the check and informed the donor that he had turned it over to "community interests." He now makes it plain generally that money so obtained will not be used to support him personally, but is for the parish.

Dean Ray lives in a pleasant gray-stone building in Twenty-ninth Street, next to his church. He writes letters and attends to weddings, funerals, and christenings in the morning, goes for little walks and pays calls and performs other parish duties and more weddings in the afternoon, and in the evening has people to dinner or dines out and goes to the theater, or stays at home and goes to sleep. He dislikes exercise and cold water, cannot remember names, and keeps his weight down by working in the garden in a rubber corset on his hundred-and-thirty-acre place at Litchfield. It takes him a week, in the

intervals between his other duties, to compose his
sermons. His favorite theme is that no matter how
insuperable seem the odds against a man, they can
be overcome by courage. He thinks Compton Mac-
kenzie is the greatest living author and is also fond
of detective fiction and the writings of Mrs. Whar-
ton. He eats a lot and likes foods that are highly seasoned, such as old Roquefort cheese—the older the
better.

If these details, lumped together, make him seem
like a medieval friar in modern clothes, it should be
recorded that he lacks at once the hearty sensuality
and the capacity for spite depicted in Chaucer's
churchmen, and that he has tolerance and social tact,
two virtues which are peculiar to highly civilized
people. He is a good host and an agreeable guest;
although be no longer acts in amateur theatricals, he
keeps up his connection with the stage in other ways.
He belongs to the Lambs and the Players and is one
of the founders of an organization called the Episcopal Actors' Guild, the purpose of which is to raise
money for sick actors and to encourage young ones.
George Arliss, Otis Skinner, Grant Mitchell, E. H.
Sothern, and Daniel Frohman are friends of his; he
prepared the Astaires for confirmation and baptized
Peggy Wood's child. Sometimes he has Mrs. Fiske
to tea. He is on good terms with Dr. Guthrie

of St. Marks-in-the-Bouwerie and with Otto Kahn,
whom he often meets at first nights and whom he
asks for help when organizing his occasional campaigns to raise money for his parish.

Besides his interest in the stage, he differs from
most other Episcopal high churchmen in his anxiety
about our future here on earth. The Bible, to be sure,
provides certain assurances regarding that part of
the future which presumably follows death, but it
gives man no way of finding out what lies ahead during his corporeal lifetime. Accordingly Dean Ray has
turned for help to Mrs. Evangeline Adams, the
astrologer, whom he has known for twenty years.
He met her when, newly ordained, he was about to
go out to Texas to the agricultural college and was
wondering how his future in the ministry was going
to work out. When Mrs. Adams set up an establishment a few blocks from a hotel where he was stay-
ing, he paid her five dollars to predict his future.
Mrs. Adams asked him the date of his birth and a
few other questions and then began to prophesy.

"You are going on a trip," she said in a low voice,
"a long, long trip. It will turn out well, but not the
way you think, because . . . something is going
to happen. Something is going to happen to somebody very dear to you. You will return from your
trip. I can see that. You will return to the place

from which you started. Later you will occupy a position of importance in a great community."

. When he got home Dr. Ray wondered how she had known that he was going on a trip. He was further amazed at her clairvoyance when his father—obviously the dear person referred to—died of a stroke of paralysis a short time later. Certainly her statements about returning from his trip and occupying a position of importance must have meant coming back to New York from Texas as rector of the Little Church Around the Corner. Since the first séance he has consulted Mrs. Adams often. When she married a chap named Arnold he performed the ceremony in his church. She has foretold all that will happen to him and his wife and daughter. So thoroughly does Dean Ray understand and admire Mrs. Adams's theories that when they are questioned he frequently defends them.

"If the moon has an influence on the tides, as we all know it has, I really don't see why the other planets might not influence our lives, do you?"

Since any answer to this question seems unnecessary, Dean Ray does not expect one. From his neat desk in his little study he stares out of the window as though to pierce beyond the pink silk curtains the somber mysteries that bound the lives of comfortable vicars.

SILK AND LEATHER

SILK AND LEATHER

WHEN Earl Sande won the Kentucky Derby on Zev in 1923, and when he won it again last spring on Gallant Fox photographs were taken of him and the horses—the sort of photograph that is always taken of a Derby winner: the horse, looking slim and easy, in the winner's circle at Churchill Downs; a man holding the bridle, and Sande, smiling, with a big bundle of roses in his arms. His rather wide, small, reddened face, peaked cap, and large ears poked out stiffly from above the flowers.

Seeing the photographs, you could provide the rest of the scene. The crowd in the stands would still be clapping and shouting; along the rail, on stamped earth littered with torn betting tickets, men with field glasses slung round them would be trying to see over each other's heads; the band would be playing, and the numbers would still show on the board. At these moments a jockey seems an important and memorable figure, but I don't think many people are misled by photographs of Derby winners into supposing that a jockey's life is mainly a matter of receiving bouquets. It is hard, dangerous, and not very well paid. The prescribed fee for a ride is ten dollars a losing mount and twenty-five dollars a winner. Of course, the owners don't stick to that —they give presents. Many of the best jockeys make from fifteen thousand to twenty thousand dollars a year. Sande makes close to fifty thousand.

Being the highest paid jockey, he has a good chance to show off like the riders of the 'eighties and 'nineties, jockeys who lived in a flashy way, bet big money on themselves, and bought champagne when they won. But Sande is quiet. He never finds much to say to strangers. One betting man who tried for half an hour to make him talk about coming winners was thoughtful as he left Sande's house.

"Say," he said to the man who had introduced him, "your boy friend Sande is dumb, isn't he?"

"Oh, I don't know."

"He's dumb, all right. Every time I mentioned a horse he'd say, 'Yes, that's a good horse.' Finally I said, 'I guess they're all good horses, Mr. Sande,' and he said, 'Yes, they have to be good.' He's dumb, all right. He's dumb like a fox."

Sande is quiet when he is riding. He is what is known as a hand rider. Even when he steps away from the bunch to win a spectacular race in the last part of the stretch you won't see him lean out to whale a horse with the whip; his hands are what make it move. And in his personal life he has so little to say that you think him stupid until you realize that his intelligence is a specialized kind of muscular strategy, useful for the single purpose of getting a horse through a race. He can't analyze this quality and wouldn't know he had it if he didn't see its results. He has no talent for exploiting himself. He would have been happy and efficient as a bank clerk, but he would never have got a raise unless the bank caught fire or some situation came about in which he could show his ability to act quickly and resist excitement. There are lots of men like Earl Sande in the world. His brother, for instance, had the same sort of coördination that he has, but his brother could never ride race horses. He was too big. Now he runs a clothing store in Salem, Oregon.

Earl Sande now is not much bigger than his big brother was when the Sande family, early in the century, moved from Groton, South Dakota, to American Falls, Idaho. Mr. Sande senior was a fair-sized Norwegian who bossed a section gang for the Milwaukee Railroad. The men who worked for him thought he was Scotch because, as does his son now, he pronounced his name "Sandy." The boys went to school in American Falls. Earl wanted a pony.

When he was fourteen he traded some live ducks and a shotgun for a little roan named Babe.

There weren't many good horses in American Falls. A man named Burr Scott had the best, a couple of racing cold bloods (horses that are half thoroughbreds). He had seen Sande ride Babe in some pick-up races. On the Fourth of July, which was celebrated in American Falls with some sprints and a rodeo, he paid him two dollars to ride Guise, one of the cold bloods. Sande won that race and later rode other races for Burr Scott, a shiftless, adventuring man, but one who knew horses.

That winter Earl went back to school. One day in spring a boy passed him a note which said that someone outside was asking for him. He got excused and went out. Burr Scott was sitting in a buckboard behind which his two race horses were tied on a lead rope.

"I thought I'd take a trip through Arizona," the man said; "there's plenty of racing there. If you came with me we might make some money."

A few weeks later Sande wrote to his family from Phoenix, Arizona. He explained how he had come to run away; Burr Scott's offer, he said, had seemed like a chance it would be bad to miss. The trip had not turned out as well as they expected. The cold bloods lost races, and Scott had been forced

to sell them in Phoenix and go home. Sande got a job
galloping horses at twenty-five cents apiece from a
veterinary named Doc Pardee, who ran a livery
stable in Phoenix and owned two race horses, Vanity
Fair and Tic-Tac. Pardee, too, lost money and sold
his horses, but when Sande left he gave him a letter
to a man named Goodman, who bought Sande's
contract from Pardee and sold it again to Johnson
& Kane, a stable in New Orleans. Sande rode for
Johnson & Kane that winter at thirty dollars a
month. When spring came he moved North with the
horses and raced on the Kentucky tracks. He rode a
hundred and fifty-eight winners. Commander
J. K. L. Ross, the Canadian, bought his contract
and doubled his pay.

Sande was getting a reputation, taking his place
with other famous jockeys, Lawrence Lyke and
Pony McAtee, Andy Schuttinger, Frankie Keogh,
who also rode for Ross, and Frank Robinson, who
was killed in a spill at Bowie. When he was not riding he used to go over and watch the start, studying
the tactics of the riders and listening to the starter's
talk.

"Move over, Joe—move over Number Seven—
bring him back—on the Salmon entry . . . I'm telling you to back him; hold it, hold it."

When they went away he watched them grow

small and string out and heard across the field the noise in the stands as they turned into the stretch. His favorite mount was Billy Kelly, a brown gelding, fast and clever. He still says he liked Billy Kelly better than any other horse he ever rode, but when someone asks him to tell why he liked him so much Sande gets tongue-tied. "Well," he says, "he was a good horse. Smart. As smart as most men, I guess. He had plenty of speed. Of course, I like all good horses."

He rode Man o' War once, in the Miller Stakes at Saratoga. He agrees with most other people that Man o' War was the fastest, strongest horse ever bred in this country. When Sir Barton, one of Ross's horses, ran against Man o' War, Sande was picked to ride Sir Barton. Just before the race he found that Keogh had the horse. Sande went to see Commander Ross.

"Didn't you want me to ride to-day, Mr. Ross?" he asked.

"You let Frankie take him, Earl," said the owner. "You're in an unlucky streak lately."

Sande was so angry he felt sick. He asked for his contract and went to work for Mr. Harry Sinclair of the Rancocas Stables.

The fact that Ross would not let him ride Sir Barton at the last minute looked bad, but Ross was only acting on a "hunch." Sande is famous for always trying to win. The horses he rides are short-priced favorites partly because they are good horses and partly because he is riding them.

Even if his mount seems out of it Sande makes him work. Once, on Salacious, he was left flat-footed at the post. The last of the field was ten lengths in front of him before he could get his horse to start. At three eighths of a mile he had caught the trailers, at the half he was up with the second division, he was in the bunch as they started the stretch, and he finished two lengths in front.

In one year the horses he rode for Sinclair earned $564,000 in stakes. He and the other Rancocas star, Laverne Fator, worked together cleverly. Whoever was on the fast horse would take him out in front, bearing out a little at the turn so that the other, on a horse that was a strong finisher, would have room to push past along the rail and win.

Sande was the only jockey who knew how to get the best out of brown Mad Hatter, a horse so temperamental that to make him go faster the rider had to pretend to pull him, and to give him his head if he wanted to slow up. And there was a day at Churchill Downs with Zev when Sande, who had got away in front, thought his horse was quitting. The leaders of the big field, bunched up and moving smoothly, the jocks flattened down, working their legs like frogs, came into the straightaway where the crowd was packed so close that people leaned, shouting, over the rail almost against the horses. Sande, on the inside, was afraid for the first time in his life to stay there. He was afraid Zev would collide with one of the faces pushed out at him. He was still in front, but the little swerve made him lose ground; Martingale, behind, was trying to press through the opening he had left, and Nassau, the favorite, was moving up on the left. In two hundred yards the race would be over, in a hundred and fifty Zev would be beaten. The jockey could feel the long, pulling bound of the horse shorten, tire; he hit Zev with his whip. Sande does not count on the whip in his rides, does not know how to use it very well, but this time the three-year-old straightened out and Sande found himself being photographed in the winner's circle with a bunch of roses.

This race is worth remembering because such high stakes and honors went with winning it, but there is a good story in almost any horse race. Sande has won so many it is hard to keep track of them. He won the Derby another time with Flying Ebony, he won the Belmont stakes four times, the Suburban handicap three times, the Metropolitan Handicap twice with Mad Hatter. He has been second in the

Futurity three times and now wants to win this race more than any other. In 1925 he estimated that he had brought in 718 winners out of 2,680 starts. Since then he has not counted up, but the number of his winners might be reckoned at the same percentage. He rides about three hundred races a year; almost all the best American horses of the last ten years have been trusted to him at one time or another— Stromboli, Exterminator, Sir Barton, Cudgel, Purchase, Thunderclap, Grey Lag, Valoris, Mad Play, Sarazen. He doesn't talk about them much. Some jockeys like to discuss their races; they get excited and wave their hands around, telling you just what happened. But Sande, if asked how he won or lost, will say something like, "Well, I got away third and I kept back until the turn and then I brought him along. He had a lot left, that horse."

In the old days he often rode the card—six races a day.

Now Sande has taken on too much weight for that, for the majority of the horses carry light imposts. Weighing in before a race, in a costume that weighs about as much as a show girl's—silk shirt and twill breeches, riding boots as light as dancing slippers, and carrying a pommel-pad saddle, and blinkers which add up to one pound, he weighs 115—a big weight for a jockey. Sometimes a day goes by in which there is not a race that he is light enough to ride in. He works hard keeping down—goes out running in sweaters and a rubber suit, takes Turkish baths. He only eats two meals a day. One of these is toast, fruit, and coffee.

In 1924, at Saratoga, Sande was badly hurt. He was edging through an opening next the rail when a young jockey, trying for the same place, cut over in front of him. There was only room for one horse and rider in the opening and Sande, to save the boy, pulled out; his horse, struck from behind and sideways, fell. The young jockey didn't fall, but when the horses had passed over the place the crowd saw Sande lying in the track beside a horse which, looking odd with its long, outstretched neck and empty saddle, was trying to knee itself up. As the field finished, the ambulance sputtered out, bumping over the rough midway, and the people in the stands, overcome with the embarrassment that follows accidents, stared while the stretcher was lifted in.

Next day the papers said that Sande's thigh had been broken close to the hip. He was so weak from taking off weight that it took him a long time to get well. While he lay sick the talk got round that he would never ride again.

Someone, I think it was Kipling, wrote a story about a cavalry colonel who dreamed that he had fallen off his horse and that the hoofs of his mounted regiment, charging behind him, beat over him as he lay helpless. One turfman suggested to me that perhaps Sande, since his fall, was troubled by some nightmare like this. This might be, but I don't think so. He seems too healthy, and he works too hard. He gets up at five-thirty in the morning and goes out to the track to see the horses exercised, comes home, eats breakfast, reads the paper, goes out to the track at one-thirty, works till five or six, comes home for dinner, and tries to be in bed by ten-thirty. In the racing season he hasn't much time to see his friends. In the winters he does not ride but goes West to see his family. He doesn't smoke or drink. He likes to listen to the radio and plays a little golf. He has no children.

Sande still has a few active years ahead of him. He says that when his muscles begin to stiffen up and the fight against weight seems no use he will stop riding and become a trainer. He will make a good trainer, I think, and I can see how he will look, standing beside the track in the morning with a watch in his hand while the exercise boys take out the horses. But although I have seen little Sande buttoned into elegant, stiff store-clothes, I always think of him as he looked on Gallant Fox on Derby Day, parading past the grand stand in the sunshine while the pari-mutuel windows rattled down. As the horses, with their hooded heads and long, rabbit-like haunches, moved by in a line, Sande never looked at the crowd but sat 'way up on the withers so that even in the walk to the barrier his weight would not be on the horse's back. He looked quiet and as if he had no doubts, and I remembered what his quietness and reticence make you forget sometimes—that he is a great jockey, one of the greatest that ever lived, and one who always tries to win.

THE LITTLE HEINIE

THE LITTLE HEINIE

LOU GEHRIG has accidentally got himself into
a class with Babe Ruth and Dempsey and
other beetle-browed, self-conscious sluggers
who are the heroes of our nation. This is ridiculous
—he is not fitted in any way to have a public. I don't
think he is either stimulated or discouraged by the
reactions of the crowds that watch his ponderous
antics at first base for the Yankees or cheer the hits
he knocks out with startling regularity and almost
legendary power. He enjoys playing ball and indicates his enjoyment by grinning at everyone he
sees and occasionally running around four bases on
a diamond-shaped field, his big calves pumping
methodically under his baggy pants, bulging in an
outer as well as inside curve like those of football
players in old drawings. Aside from baseball his
principal amusement is fishing, and his principal
associates are his mother and Babe Ruth. Mrs.
Gehrig has exercised a good deal of care on his
upbringing—he is her only child—and it was she
who took him where he could learn the game in the
first place.

The exact spot at which the athletic career of

Louis Henry Gehrig may be said to have begun is
the Sigma Nu fraternity house of Columbia University, to the back door of which, one morning
fifteen years ago, came a man, a woman, and a boy.
The woman knocked, and when the door was opened
explained that she had come in answer to an advertisement which the manager of the fraternity house
had inserted in the papers that morning. The manager himself was called and Mrs. Gehrig answered
his questions, saying that she could do plain or fancy
cooking and that her husband would see to the
furnace and do any odd jobs that might be needed
around the place. Their clothes were old, but the
couple looked so healthy and good-natured that the
manager, who liked German cooking, asked them
to come in and, after a few more questions, hired
them. For several years after that the Sigma Nu
brothers enjoyed very good meals. They became used
to having Mrs. Gehrig in the kitchen and to the
presence there with her, at certain times of day, of
her eleven-year-old boy who went to day school
somewhere and came to the fraternity house, when
he had time, to help his mother with the dishes. He
was the sort of boy who laughed whenever you spoke
to him. Big for his age, he had reached the period
when the change from short to long trousers was
imminent, but he still wore short ones; their tight-

ness exaggerated the size of his fat round legs. Sometimes fraternity brothers who were having a catch in the yard after supper let him get in it. He threw well and liked to play ball.

As time passed, things changed at the Sigma Nu house. The man who had been manager graduated; the Gehrigs left too, after a while, in answer to an advertisement promising favorable conditions to a couple who would cook and look after a furnace. During the next six years the boy, who had been referred to as "the little Heinie" by the fraternity brothers, ate quantities of good food cooked by his mother. At sixteen he was in his last year in the High School of Commerce and had already attained his present weight of two hundred and thirty pounds when his school was given permission to use the Columbia field for one of its games. Among the high-school rooters, a little group of girls with feathers and pennants, and boys with ostentatious cigarettes, sitting on the lower benches of the big, empty stands, was the athletic director of the university—the same fellow who a few years before had managed the Sigma Nu fraternity house. He had come down to the field principally to pass away a tedious afternoon and, remotely, in the hope of seeing some football material. He had made up his mind to go round to the showers after the game and ask the big full back of the High School of Commerce where he was going to college, when somebody touched his arm and he found himself confronted by a stocky, vaguely familiar man with blue eyes and a gray mustache. Phrases of greeting, pronounced in a German accent, prompted his memory —Gehrig, the fellow who had looked after the furnace at the frat house. The full back of the High School of Commerce was his own son, the former furnace man informed the director—didn't he remember Lou, the little Heinie?

The coincidence of their old acquaintanceship, together with the arguments advanced by the athletic director when he found the little Heinie in the showers, resulted in procuring another presumable football star for Columbia. By the following autumn Lou Gehrig, in a pair of old pants and a white shirt, was a familiar figure on the campus. He had not been ready at first to take Columbia entrance exams, but six rather painful months in the extension school had got him by. He continued to get by for two years, and meanwhile played right tackle with some distinction, working out at baseball in the spring—for a while at first base and then as varsity pitcher. One spring afternoon, in a college game, he hit the longest homer that any Columbia, perhaps any under-graduate, player had ever made

—more than four hundred feet. Reports of this hit brought some scouts from professional teams to see him, and before the season was over several teams had made him offers.

Whether he ought to turn professional harassed the Gehrig family until it was decided. For the most part the argument was between Lou and his mother —the old man kept out of it, yet in a way it was his future, and not Lou's, that they were arguing about. He had been sick that winter and needed an operation. Accepting the Yankees' contract would bring in more than enough money for everything they needed; that was a strong argument, but for a while Mrs. Gehrig held out against it. Baseball had always been and still is for her a mysterious and somewhat nonsensical business. Having her son a student at Columbia was something palpable, a glory that her experience made appear as probably exceeding anything else that could happen to him. Even now, although on occasion she goes to the stadium, and nods her head in a pleased way over her son's achievements, it is that period at college that seems most splendid to her. When talking about him with strangers she calls him Columbia Lou—jokingly, of course—but just to remind them, in case they didn't know. . . .

Mr. Gehrig's operation was duly paid for with

the first money Lou earned in the big leagues—or
almost in the big leagues, for the Yankees farmed
him out for a year to Hartford. It wasn't until
1924, when they took him South for training, that
he made the acquaintance of players whose deeds he
had read about and whose batting averages he had
known by heart since high school and before. He
experienced then for the first time the peculiar atmosphere of a major-league ball club. It may as well
be admitted that he did not fit into his new environment with much grace.

So much has been written about the way seasoned
ball players kid rookies that I will not go into the
matter here except to note that Gehrig's team mates
remember him in those days as one of the most
bewildered recruits that ever joined the club. He
conformed in every detail to what tradition laid down
as expected of rookies—the paper suitcase, the confidence, the grin, the store suit, the letters to his
mother. He was slow-witted—could find no come-
back for the wisecracks directed at him—and his
schoolboyish peculiarities were an inspiration to the
team wits and a source of worry to Manager Miller
Huggins. Going without an overcoat, hat, or waistcoat, for instance, was all right in Florida, but when
he was leaving the stadium one raw spring day
without these civilized protections, a team official

stopped him and pressed a hundred-dollar bill into his hand.

"Take this, Lou. You can fix me up later."

"What for?" demanded Gehrig.

"Go down and buy yourself some clothes," the other stated firmly. "I see you're in a hole. You can pay me back—any time will be all right."

Gehrig refused the money, explaining that he saved all his salary and had plenty but that he never wore a vest or overcoat because they made him feel dressed up. He persisted in this theory until about a year ago when, to avoid the conspicuousness attending his increasing fame, he began to dress like other people.

Few of the players who used to kid Gehrig in his early days with the Yankees failed to get on well with him, but several stars on other teams found him irritating. One of them was Ty Cobb. Gehrig symbolized to Cobb just what a ball player ought not to be—a slugger, a rube, offensive for all his traits, including his good nature. Whenever the Yankees played Detroit, Cobb would make Gehrig sore by calling him a thick-headed Dutchman. He repeated this phrase monotonously as he trotted past the big first-baseman at the end of every inning. Every time Detroit was in the field and Gehrig reached second base, Cobb moved in a little and, bent forward with his hands on his knees, directed a flow of remarks at him out of the corner of his mouth.

"Keep your foot on the bag, Wiener Schnitzel. Go on back there, you thick-headed Dutch bum."

Either such comparatively harmless insults got on Gehrig's nerves by sheer repetition, or Cobb by degrees put more bite in them. One day, as a game ended, the two started a fight in the Tigers' dugout. Charging at his tormentor, who stepped deftly out of range, Gehrig hit his head on a stanchion of the low roof and fell down stunned. By the time he got up, other players surrounded the two and kept them apart. Next day they shook hands. Cobb seemed to like Gehrig for having nerve enough to try to hit him.

Gehrig's relations with Babe Ruth were more equable. The Babe, whom he idolized at long range during his college days, was nice to him on first acquaintance, watched him develop without jealousy, and helped him whenever he could. He even taught him to play bridge, and in games in the Yankees' private car on trips they are generally partners. Playing for money made Gehrig learn quickly. When, after some preliminary coaching, he sat down to his first real game, the matter of stakes did not seem important.

"What will it be, Lou?" an opponent asked. "Is one cent too much?"

"One cent—it don't have to be as low as that."

The stake was fixed at five cents. On the second hand Gehrig bid, and went down three hundred.

"That cost you fifteen bucks," Ruth, his partner, told him gently.

"Fifteen bucks!" exclaimed Gehrig. "My golly! This is a smart game."

By application he made his bridge game better just as he did his fielding. Miller Huggins figured him as a natural first-baseman and built him up carefully until, in 1925, he replaced Wally Pipp as a regular. He now covers his base effectively and generally throws the ball to the right place, although emergencies are still apt to upset him. Huggins had trouble training him but says that Gehrig's lack of conceit made him a good pupil; he took orders obediently, learned slowly, but never forgot an idea once he understood it. At bat he hits the ball farther on an average than Ruth. Two years ago he kept up with the Babe until August in a home-run contest followed eagerly even by people who rarely went to ball games. By degrees Gehrig fell behind, finishing with forty-seven to Ruth's sixty. Last year he only had twenty-seven to Ruth's fifty-two, but made up for it by driving in nine runs in the World Series and tying Ruth's record of four homers for the series. He incidentally tied a former long-standing record of .545 for a World Series batting average. He isn't as fast on bases or as good a fielder or as big a drawing card as Ruth. He makes about twenty-four thousand a year.

Repeatedly Ruth and Gehrig, sometimes with successive home runs, have won games that seemed lost. The most impressive hitting they ever did was not in a game at all but during batting practice in Pittsburgh before the World Series of 1927. The double-decker bleachers of the Pittsburgh stand curve around behind right field; Huggins told Ruth and Gehrig to see how man balls they could get in the upper bleachers. First Ruth bounced six long drives against the empty seats, then Gehrig dropped four or five in the same place. The Pirates watched in amazement the two greatest batters in the world reaching nonchalantly a spot that they had hardly touched all season. It is reasonable to think that the exhibition did not improve their confidence. Anyway, the Yankees took the series in straight games.

With his share of the profits of two successful World Series, Gehrig bought a house in New Rochelle, where he lives with his parents. It is a neat white wooden house in a residential district, set back from the road in an oblong lawn shaded with

trees—some pines in front of the porch, and two
or three big elms in the yard behind. A fine place,
certainly, but in some ways Gehrig misses Morningside Park, where the family went to live when he began to make money. The kids in Morningside Park
were always playing ball, and when he drove home
from the stadium in his Chevrolet he would run into
the apartment and leave his coat and come out and
play with them.

Sometimes in the winter one of the Yankees asks
him down South to hunt or fish. When he is at home
he gets up early and plays with the dogs. The
Gehrigs' house is full of pets: there are a parrot, two
canaries, a small German black-and-tan dog that
was the Yankees' mascot in the World's Series with
St. Louis, and a big black police dog that was
brought from Germany and can understand only
German. Old Mr. Gehrig won't let anyone find out
the name of this dog. He feels that if people outside
the family knew what his name was he wouldn't be
their dog any more—he would be everybody's dog.

Lou does not smoke or drink. It was recently
rumored that he had been seen at a movie theater
with a red-cheeked German girl who wore a bunch
of flowers in her hat, but this could not be verified.
When asked if he is going to get married he says,
"My mother makes a home comfortable enough for

me," and Mrs. Gehrig, if she is around, laughs as though to reprove him, nodding her head up and down. She is continually cooking for him, making apple cake, and cookies with raisins and pieces of bright red suet in them, making roasts, and frying the fish and eels he catches in the Sound. Lou goes fishing for eels so often that sometimes there are too many to eat; then Mrs. Gehrig pickles them. There is a superstitious belief among the Yankees that eating pickled eels at the Gehrigs' will make you hit the ball; if any member of the team is batting badly he tries to get Lou to ask him up to dinner. Even the largest parties at suppertime do not annoy Mrs. Gehrig.

"There is enough for everybody," she says, counting the heads, and pushing chairs up to the table.

"Why should Lou eat eels?" some ball player remarks later, wiping his mouth. "He always hits good, doesn't he, Mr. Gehrig?"

Pushed back a little from the table sits Father Gehrig, a square-cut, solid figure; he smokes a pipe, and the smoke swings up and hangs in the air.

"*Ja,*" he answers. "That's right *Ja* . . . *Ja* . . . *Ja.*"

THE END